Chapter 1

"Honey. Honey," I hear someone saying while simultaneously shaking me. "It's about that time."

I open my eyes and see the most beautiful woman in the world staring down at me.

"Good morning Dr. Jenkins", she says.

"Good morning Mrs. Dr. Jenkins,"

She leans down and kisses my forehead.

"That's my move," I say frowning.

She laughs.

"Breakfast is almost ready. Hurry up so we can eat."

"Yes mam," I say standing up. "Where's Kennedy?"

No sooner had I said her name; Kennedy runs into the bedroom.

"Morning daddy," she says leaping into my arms.

"Good morning my angel."

She hugs my neck and gives me a big kiss on the jaw.

"Guess what daddy," she says.

"What."

"My birthday is in three days," she says holding up three fingers.

"Oh my God," I say matching her excitement. "My baby is getting old. Pretty soon it's going to be time for you to get a job."

"No daddy," she says smiling. "Mommy doesn't have a job. I'm going to be like her."

"Mommy does have a job. She has the most important job. She makes sure we are taking care of. I don't know what I would do without her."
I looked at Nicole. She was blushing. I always marveled at how red her dark cheeks could become.

"Flattery will get you nowhere Dr. Jenkins. Come on mam," Nicole says reaching for Kennedy. "We have to finish breakfast."

"Nooooo I'm not ready," Kennedy says squeezing my neck tighter.

I couldn't breathe, however I couldn't let her see me choke. I broke her grip and told her to go with her mom. She went reluctantly.

"Ok mommy. I'm ready now," she said.

I watched them leave. I'm not sure, but I have the strangest suspicion Nicole added a little something extra to her walk because she knew I was watching.

It didn't take long for me to get dressed. I was eager to have breakfast with my family. They were in the dining room. Sitting at the table. We always eat breakfast together. A tradition that started when Kennedy was born.

"I don't know what you cooked, but it smells good," I say.

"I'm glad you think so. We tried a new recipe. I hope you like it," Nicole said walking into the kitchen.

"Daddy," Kennedy says.

"Yes mam."

"I helped mommy cook. We put strawberries in the pancakes."

"I love strawberries. I'm excited to try your pancakes."
Kennedy smiled brightly. Nicole walked back into dining room with my plate.

"Mommy daddy said he's excited to try my pancakes."

"Did he," Nicole says. "Well here you go daddy."
She sat my plate in front of me.
Kennedy laughed.

"He's not your daddy mommy. He's my daddy."
Nicole smirked at me.

"You're right baby. He's your daddy and your daddy alone.'
After returning with plates for herself and Kennedy; Nicole sat down so we could begin eating.

"Oh wow. These are good," I say to Kennedy after taking my first bite.

Kennedy smiled. She was clearly pleased with herself.

"So Dr. Jenkins," Nicole says. "How many patients do you have today?"

"Three. One this morning and two after lunch."

"That's not too bad."

"What about you two? What are my favorite ladies doing today?"

"I'm your favorite princess," Kennedy chimed in.

"Yes you are," I say reaching over tickling her. "The best princess in the history of princesses."

"Daddy stop," Kennedy said laughing. I look over at Nicole. She's smiling. I smile back.

"We are grocery shopping and we have gymnastics," Nicole says.

"Isn't gymnastics a Tuesday activity," I ask.

"Yes, but your daughter wanted extra lessons."

I look at Kennedy. She's no long smiling.

"I just can't get the back hand spring. It's hard daddy."

I reach out to caress her arm.

"I understand, but I know you're going to get it. You can do whatever you put your mind to."

She smiles again. I tickle her again.

"Stop daddy," She says laughing.

We finish breakfast. I kiss them both. They wish me a good day and I walk to the bus stop.

The bus stop is less than a mile from the house. The walk there is pleasant. The early days of Spring. A homeless man asks for change. Unfortunately I don't carry cash. I explain to it to him. He smiles and says he carries credit cards. I laugh at his joke.

"Good morning," I say as I arrive at the bus stop.

"Good morning," A few of the people say.

"Jenkins what say you," I hear a familiar voice say.

I look up to see Regonal Jones III walking towards me.

Newspaper under his arm.

"Mr. Jones, good morning."

We shake hands.

"How are you this morning," he asked.

"I'm fine. Woke up to a beautiful woman and an angel. So I'm doing pretty well."

"I agree. Wonderful way to wake up," he says. "If you have time; let's do lunch this week. There are some things I want to discuss with you."

"Sure. Have your secretary contact Charlie to set it up."

Mr. Jones laughed.

"I should be offended that you pawned me off to your assistant, but I know if you had to do it; it would never happen.

I smile slightly.

"I'll have Samantha call Charlie," he said.

"Good."

I sat in silence until the bus arrived. I usually sit in the middle of the bus. Doing so allows me to get the best sense of what's going on. I take a seat next to an elderly gentleman. He smiled as I sat down. I returned his smile. He returned to looking out the window.

"That's the most asinine thing I've heard in a long time," the gentleman across from me said.
I noticed he had on a sweat shirt that said 'I only date black women'. I wondered where he bought it. The gentlemen in front of me laughed. He was wearing a red hat

"Of course you feel that way," he said. "You're another weak black man that panders to black women and refuses to say what needs to be said. You are the type of brother than will see a woman doing the most absurd thing possible and will find a way to blame black men for her behavior."

"So I'm weak because I don't place the blame of the plight of the black community on the shoulders of black men? It makes me weak to expect black men to lead?"

"No you're weak because you won't be honest about black women."
The guy with the sweater shakes his head.

"So what's the truth about black women? This should be good."

"I'm glad you asked," Red hat says. "Black women have no integrity or dignity or self respect. Just prices. Nowadays all they want to do is listen to Cardi B and watch reality shows."
He shook his head.

"It's sad," he continued. "The level of mental retardation we are witnessing. All for some damn materials."

"Wow," I say aloud.
He turned around, looked at me, and smiled.

"That's false," The guy with the sweater says. "Categorizing black women in that manner is dangerous and just plain stupid. What you're saying does in fact apply to some black women; a very small percentage, but not all. You made an all inclusive statement. I will not allow you to talk about black women in such a negative manner. It's sad that it's black men that are the primary source of hatred for black women.

He shook his head.

"It really be your own people," he finished.

Red hat laughs.

"Of course you're going to say that. Weak ass black man."

"I'm weak because I believe in protecting black women from the abuse they receive from black men? I'm weak because I see black women as the treasures they are? If that makes me weak; I'll gladly accept being weak. You're the reason the black community is in shambles.

Majority of you are felons, about to be felons, broke and don't care to fix it or you refuse to be faithful. It's no wonder black women are turning to each other and men of other races for companionship."

"You do realize you're a black man right?"
Good question I thought to myself.

"Oh yes I know I'm black. I'm a good black man, but for every one of me there are 30 to 40 of you ain't shit men."
There were a lot of people watching their exchange. I could tell some wanted to chime in but decided against it. I shared their sentiment.

"If black women are such jewels," Red Hat started. "Explain to me the crack epidemic or those little boys that watch their moms work three jobs, cook and clean for them, but turn out gay. Explain to me why these baby mamas don't allow black men to see their children. All because he doesn't want to be with her anymore. You clearly have all the answers when it comes to black women. Explain that to me."

I was confused about how he drew that correlation.

"What does the crack epidemic or little boys growing up to be gay have to do with anything," the guy with the sweatshirt asked. "Are you really blaming black women for the crack epidemic? I'm done talking to you."

"You need to overstand matriarch and patriarch relationships."

"You're one of those people that claim to be enlightened because you're read a few more books that everyone else, but instead of using what you've learned to uplift people; you use that information to beat people over the head. You proclaim to have achieved a higher level of consciousness, but you're acting just like the racists that persecute us. You're no better than the judge that gives lil Timmy 30 years for stealing food. You may be woke but you're so woke that you need a nap."

I laughed at the joke, but I also was in agreeance with what he said. I also found it hypocrital that he would say that. In large part because he spent the last twenty minutes throwing black men under the proverbal bus. The pot called the kettle black. The two gentlemen continued their conversation. I was quickly losing interest.

"I know what your problem is," the woman next to sweatshirt said.

"Oh great another black woman telling a black man what his problem is, but doesn't know what her problem is. What's my problem? Please tell me my problem," Red hat says pretentiously.

"For one you're ignorant, but you major problem is that you don't like women."
Red hat laughed.

"See what did I tell you," he said. "Black women act like they know everything, but don't know anything.

Nothing about me is gay. I actually despise gay black men."

"I didn't say you were gay. I said you don't like women. You like how we look. You like our vaginas, breasts, and asses, but you don't like us. You don't like the essence of a woman. And you know what they say about men that proclaim to hate gay men?"

"No I don't but I know you're going to tell me," Red hat said rolling his eyes.

"Straight men," she said using air quotes."That claim to hate gay men are secretly gay themselves. It's ok sis we accept you."
The bus erupted in laughter. Red hat was saying something, however I couldn't hear him over the laughter.

"You tell him black woman," Sweater said.

"You're not off the hook either," She said turning to him.

"What do you mean," he asked. There was a look of confusion on his face.

"Look man. I appreciate you for sticking up for black women. God knows we need more black men to, but you don't have to turn down black men to build us up."

"I didn't."

"Yes sir you did. You said majority of black men are no good. And my brother that's just not true. It's actually the exact opposite. Majority of black men are good brothers; strong, hardworking, productive members of society."

"Not according to statistics."

"You can't be referring to statistics that are created and generated by the dominant society," she said laughing. "I know that's not your source. I'll be the first to admit that there are some low down no good brothers, however those are the exceptions. Not the rule. You're coming off as a hater."

"Hater," Sweater said in disbelief. "How am I hating?"

"You're tearing down other black men to make yourself look better."

"No I'm not."

"Yes you are. You literally said that women have to go through 40 dudes that aren't about nothing before they find a good man like you. You're a man sweaty. I'm sure you're violating mancode."

"Mancode is a bunch of rubbish", sweater said with a hint of disgust in his voice.

"You don't have many male friends do you?"
He didn't say anything.

"I didn't think so. You probably were raised in a household dominated by women too.
He still didn't say anything.

"Sweetie, I'm going to need you to get you some male friends," she said rubbing his shoulder. "Not ones like Mr. I Hate Women over There, but brothers that are

mentally healthy. Understand"

"Yes mam," Sweater said.

Red hat chimed in and the heated discussion resumed.

"That's the problem." The older gentleman next to

me says aloud to himself.

I look at him. He's looking at me.

"Black people are divided," he continued. "Half of

you are more concerned with who's to blame or getting

others to see your plight that you're unable to find a

solution. We all know there's racism, discrimination, and a

host of other disadvantages black people are faced with,

however continuing to talk about them does very little to

overcome them."

"What do you think the solution is," I ask.

He smiles.

"It's not that simple. There isn't one solution. You're facing multiple issues so you're going to need multiple solutions. A multifaceted response to the multifaceted attack you're experiencing.

"Attack," I say.

"Yes attack. You people have been under attack every since we re-entered Africa.

I didn't say anything. He smiled at me.

"You didn't think a white man knew all that did you?"

"I know that white people are aware of what's going on; it surprises me to hear them admit it out loud."

"I understand. We talk about it in private, although briefly. Followed immediately by how it's your own fault and other things we say that serve as justifications. But like I was saying; you people need more economic empowerment, better education, and most important unity. That's where everything starts unity. There's no unity.

You've been divided and conquered. Until you come together; you people will always be in last place. But you don't hear me though," he said before returning his attention to the window.

Chapter 2: Christopher Hitchson

I step off the elevator, walk through the glass doors, to see a gentleman sitting in the waiting area. He's dressed in a polo style shirt and some khakis. I don't recognize him. I don't have any appointments this morning either. Charlie would know who he is.

"Good morning," I say as I approach her desk.

"Good morning doctor," She says with a smile.

"How was your morning commute?"

I pause for a moment. Thinking back to what I had heard this morning.

"It was interesting," I reply.

I look back at the gentlemen. He looks up from his cell phone and smiles at me. It was one of those nervous smiles people give you when they are in an uncomfortable situation. I smile back.

"That's Christopher Hitchson," Charlie says.

"Who," I ask.

"Christopher Hitchson. He came in this morning looking for you. He says he received your card from a friend."

"Did he say who the friend was?"

"Not exactly," she says looking at her notepad.

"You wrote notes,"

Charlie smiles.

"Of course I did. Not all of us were blessed with a perfect memory."

I didn't know if she was being condescending or stating a fact. She may not have a perfect memory, however she does possess the ability to say something really crude, without others realizing it. I attribute it to the fact that she's smiling the entire time.

"How much time before my first appointment," I ask.

"It's 8:50 now. Mrs. Porter isn't schedule to be here until 10:00. So a little over an hour."

I look back at Mr. Hitchson.

"Okay give me ten minutes and send him back."

"Yes sir," she says.

I walk back to my office. I usually spend Monday mornings reading and meditating. Unfortunately due to Mr. Hitchson's arrival, I want be able to spend my morning in the usual manner. I decide to do a quick mediation. I light a candle, write my questions down, and start my meditative breathing. Morning mediation is essential to my success.

After about 8 minutes I decide to stop. Charlie is a stickler for details; so she will send Mr. Hitchson to my office in exactly ten minutes. Not long afterwards there's a knock

on the door.

I get up to open the door.

"Good morning sir. My name is Dr. Jenkins," I say

extending my hand.

He reaches out to shake my hand.

"My name is Christopher Hitchson," he says

nervously.

He steps in the office.

"Feel free to have a seat," I say. "I know it's cliché

to have a sofa, however some of my patients are comforted

by it."

"Can I sit in the chair," he asks.

"Yes. Be my guest."

The chair is next to the couch. I sit in a chair opposite the

patient's sitting area. My desk is behind me. It's close

enough that I can get what I need quickly, but far away

enough that I don't feel cramped.

"This is a nice office," he says looking around. "It's probably the biggest I've been in."

"Thank you," I say looking around. "I didn't want an unnecessarily large office; however I needed one that allowed for everything I needed to fit in without being cramped.

Mr. Hitchson didn't say anything. He simply nodded his head as he continued to look around.

"So Mr. Hitchson What brings you in today?"

He hesitates before answering.

"Well doctor," he begins. "I need some advice."

"Oh?" I say studying his face. He is obviously troubled. "Well Mr. Hitchson I don't actually give advice."

Mr. Hitchson looked at me confused.

"I thought you were a psychiatrist." He said.

I could sense the confusion in his voice.

"I am. One of the best in the country; according to the awards on the wall and my clients, but I don't give advice. What I do offer are suggestions and provide an analysis of what you tell me. My goal is to provide an alternative way of looking at things that are troubling you; change your perception regarding what is currently troubling you or has been troubling you your entire life. Often times the situation isn't as we perceive it to be. Our confusion regarding something, whether it be a person, an incident or whatever, makes everything more or less significant than it actually is. Does that make sense?"

"Yes." Mr. Hitchson said. "But to be honest Doc. I think this is a waste of time. And by looking at your office and the watch you're wearing; I don't think I can afford you."
I laughed loudly at what he said. There was something I liked about Mr. Hitchson. Something familiar. I could tell he was an intelligent person.

"I'll be honest sir. My sessions are very expensive. Taking a page from your book; looking at your watch. I know you can't afford me. As you said. 'You're a waste of my time.' I hate wasting my time. So with that being said I have to dismiss you. Good day sir." I said staring at Mr. Hitchson.

He instantly became enraged.

"Who the hell do you think you are buddy? You can't talk to people like that. You don't know me. You don't know anything about this watch. It may not have much financial value, but it has sentimental value. My father gave it to me before he let. How dare you judge me or my watch? Ass hole." Mr. Hitchson said walking towards the door.

"Ironic isn't it?" I say taking off my glasses. "I wouldn't have taken you for someone with low self-esteem. Side note: the value of a thing is determined by the person. The cost is determined by the company selling the thing. It's a big difference. "

"What the hell are you talking about?" He says turning towards me.

"Everything you said in your little soliloquy. Have a seat and I'll explain to you what I mean." I say pointing to his original seat.

"No bruh I'm good. I'd rather stand."

"Very well Mr. Hitchson. It's ironic that you were angered by my statement; especially considering that you had previously said the same thing to me. I simply reaffirmed your thoughts and feeling about us.

"I didn't say your watch was cheap or that you'd be wasting my time."
I smiled.

"Yes sir you said exactly that. Maybe not verbally, but it was said. See Mr. Hitchson. One of my greatest strengths is that I listen when people are talking. When you actually listen to what a person is saying; you also hear what they don't say."

"What they don't say? What didn't I say? If I didn't say it then it wasn't said."

Mr. Hitchson was obviously confused, but I could tell he wanted answers. I smiled.

"Take a seat Mr. Hitchson and I'll explain what I mean."

He stared at me for a moment. I could see the wheels in his mind turning. He was unsure about what he should do. Eventually he sat in the chair I offered him.

"Thank you for sitting down. I hate when people stand up angrily during sessions. Whether you know it or not Mr. Hitchson, you called yourself a waste of my time and informed me that you can't afford me. You calculated my value by my material possessions."

"I didn't mean." Mr. Hitchson says attempting to cut me off.

"Mr. Hitchson allow me to finish my thought. We're men and will respect each other as such." I say looking at him.

Based on the expression on his face; I could tell he wanted to be offended, but didn't know what he could be offended about.

"As I was saying; when you verbalized the fact that you determined my value by my material possessions; I heard you say that you base your own value in your material possessions. Are you with me so far?"

"Yes." He says.

"If you place your value in your possessions; yet you drive an old beat up Chevrolet."

He looked at me confused. Undoubtedly wondering how I knew what kind of car he drove.

"I saw you drive up as I got off the bus this morning."

"You ride the bus?"

"Yes every morning, but that's not important.
What's important is that you're someone who places his
value in his material possessions, but doesn't have much.
Doesn't have the best of everything. Your material
possessions aren't good enough for you. Being that self-
esteem is defined as the confidence a person has in himself;
how can you possibly have high self-esteem or feel that
you're good enough. If you don't feel that you're good
enough for yourself; how can you possibly feel that you're
good enough for others?
Mr. Hitchson was silent for a while.

"I never thought about it that way. So you're
saying that everyone that has more than me think they are
better than me? Or more worthy than I am? Is that why rich
dudes have more confidence and more women than me?"

"Yes and no Mr. Hitchson. You think they are
better than you. The thing about people who place their
value in their material possessions is that it is superficial

and won't last. Your material possessions can be taken away from you; if that's where your value is; than guess what else can be taken from you?

"Your value."

"Correct Mr. Hitchson. So the thing to do is to value yourself because of who you are. Your value doesn't come from others. It comes from you."

"I see what you're saying. I'm going to use that in my next book."

"If people actually listened to you; they would've picked up on that a long time ago."
This seem to startle Mr. Hitchson.

"What are you talking about? People hear me when I talk."

"That's the thing Mr. Hitchson. I said listen not hear."

"That's the same thing. And why do you keep calling me Mr. Hitchson"

"Not True. They're actually quite different. That's your name isn't it? I believe in calling people by their names. "

"It is my name but you can call me Chris. Most people do."

I smile.

"I'm not most people Mr. Hitchson. My mother made sure she imputed manners into me. I treat all people with the same level of respect."

He fell silent.

"What's the difference?" He asked. "Between listen and hear."

"I'm glad you asked." I say jumping from my chair and startling Mr. Hitchson in the process.

I walk over to my book case and grab the dictionary.

"Mr. Hitchson you're going to look up the words hear and listen so you'll know the difference."

He looked puzzled.

“I know the definition.”

I laughed.

“If that were true so; I wouldn’t feel the need to have you look them.” I say handing him the dictionary.

“Once you find the word read its definition out loud please.”

It didn’t take him long to find the first word.

“Hear; to be perceived by the ear.”

“Remember that word perceive. No listen.”

He stared at me intensely.”

“What?” I asked.

“You said listen.” He said smiling.

I too smiled.

“Good one.”

It took him a few minutes to find the definition.

“Listen; to give attention with the ear. Attend closely for the purpose of hearing.”

“Very good Mr. Hitchson. Just as I thought.”

"What?" He said closing the dictionary.

"You're an intelligent young man."

Mr. Hitchson smiled.

"Thank you. How did you gather that?"

"I'll tell you at the end of today's session, but for now let's focus on the matter at hand. Hearing and listening. After you finished reading the definition for hear; I told you to remember a word. Do you remember what that word was?"

"Yes. The word was perceive."

"Yes it was. Open the dictionary and find the definition for perceive."

Mr. Hitchson did as he was instructed.

"Perceive to be conscious or aware of something."

"Very good. You can close the dictionary now. Are you able to explain the difference between hear and listen in your own words?

"I'd give it a try."

"That's all I ask."

"TO hear is to simply know someone is saying something. You're aware that they're talking. To listen is to know what they are saying. TO understand what's being said."

"Yes exactly. You can hear people speaking in a foreign language, but that doesn't mean you're able to listen to their conversation."

"Wow."

"What's the matter Mr. Hitchson?"

"Nothing really. I just never thought about it like that."

"Yes I know. I guided you to another perspective." Mr. Hitchson was quiet for a moment. He seemed to be looking for the words to properly express himself.

"Take your time," I say

"What."

"Take your time," I repeat. "You have something to say, but you just don't know how to say it."

He looked surprised.

"How did you know that," He asked.

I smile.

"Well Mr. Hitchson," I say taking off my glasses. "I'm very good at what I do."

He just looked at me. I smile at him. Encouraging him to share his thoughts.

"I've been out of rehab for about a year now."

"Have you been sober this entire time," I ask.

"Yes."

"Very Good Mr. Hitchson. I apologize for interrupting. Continue please."

"Thank you. This time last year I was depressed and slick lost. I didn't know what I was going to do with my life. I was dealing with threats from my family, the possibility of going to jail was looking over my head, I was fat, lonely, and broke. My old friends stopped wanting to hang out because I was no longer drinking. Not to mention having to deal with emotions that I use to suppress with alcohol. I was dealing with all those things without my usual method of coping."

Mr. Hitchson paused. I remained silent. He continued to look at the floor.

"But now," He continued. "I'm working, in better shape, and have a love for life that I haven't had in nearly a decade. Within this first year I've written two books and released an app. I have a better relationship with my daughter and I'm interviewing for a better job tomorrow."

"I feel like there's a 'but' coming," I say.

He looked at me.

"It shouldn't be, but I'm still lonely. I find myself going to parties and bars in hopes that I'll find a woman or new friends that I can hang with, but I'm terrible at small talk. I never know what to say. I end up just standing

there."

I raised an eyebrow.

"I know I know." Mr. Hitchson said seeing the look

on my face. "It makes no sense to meet new friends in bars.

But there is nowhere else for me to go to meet people."

"The most intelligent people I know aren't good at

small talk. They would prefer to have deep stimulating

conversations over the meaningless filler conversations."

Mr. Hitchson's eyes lit up.

"Yes exactly. I want to talk about things that

interest me. I don't really care about the small things."

"Do you know how to initial the conversation?"

"What do you mean," Mr. Hitchson asked

quizzically.

"Exactly what I said.

"I do, but I don't know if it's the best way to do it."

"Are they responsive?"

"Yes."

"Then it's the best way to do it. The thing about human interaction is that it's not complex. It's quite simple. Two people exchanging ideas and words. That's all it is." Mr. Hitchson shook his head.

"It wasn't so hard when I was drinking. I used to be able to approach anyone and just start talking. No fear. Just start talking. I wasn't worried about being rejected or anything. Man I miss that."

"They don't call it liquid courage for nothing."

"I just got that," Mr. Hitchson said laughing. I nod.

"Where you're approaching women may also play a part in your nervousness. If you're uncomfortable in a place; chances are you're going to be apprehensive about starting conversations. Where do you spend most of your time?" I ask. "When you're not working? Where do you write?"

"I spend most of my time at the bookstore."

"Is that where you are initiating conversations?"

"No."

"Why not?"

"Because there aren't people there I want to hang with."

"What are you looking to do with these people?"
Mr. Hitchson shrugged his shoulders.

"I don't know. Talk about books, have intellectual conversations, just kick it. And have nasty freaky sex." Mr. Hitchson's face lit up when he mentioned sex. I smiled at his excitement.

"You do know that smart women are the most adventurous in the bedroom right?"

"No I didn't know that,"

"You don't want to hang with people that you meet in bookstores, although the people in bookstores are more likely to enjoy the things you mentioned you're looking for in friends? Mr. Hitchson I don't have to tell you how asinine that is."

Mr. Hitchson looked back at the floor.

"Are either of your books published?"

"Yes sir." He said looking at me.

"Who published them?"

"I did."

I was confused.

"What do you mean you published them?"

"It's quite simple. I wrote the books, started a publishing company, copyrighted the books through the publishing company and did a deal with Amazon to distribute the books."

"Wow. Mr. Hitchson. I'm impressed. What are the names of your books?"

"Nerd At The Cool Table and Daddy Loves You."

"Congratulations. I hope you become more successful than you ever thought was possible."

Mr. Hitchson smiled broadly.

I glanced at my watch.

"I have about fifteen more minutes before my next session. Tell me Mr. Hitchson; how do you feel about God?

Chapter 3: Christopher Hitchson II

"What do you mean?" Mr. Hitchson asked.

"I mean exactly what I said. How do you feel about God? Is he your homie, your buddy, your pal? Do you not really rock with him? Is your him a her."

"I've actually been trying to define God for years. And when I was in rehab they told me I needed to. They said it would help fight off my demons."

"You were in Rehab." I asked.

"Yes. I went to The Harbor House last year."

"I know that place very well. It saved my life."

Mr. Hitchson looked at me with a look of surprise.

"You went to the Harbor House?"

"Yes. About twenty years ago, but that's not important right now. What have you come up with?

"I don't know how to define him."

"So, your God is a him. What did your mom teach you about God?"
Mr. Hitchson paused.

"How do you know that it wasn't my father that taught me about God?"

"I didn't know. Not until this moment. Your mannerisms gave signs that your father was not a major factor in your upbringing. But we aren't talking about that right now. We are talking about you and God."
This seem to anger him.

"Man, I don't know. I've been trying to find the answer. Why are you asking so many questions about God? Are you some type of Jesus freak?" Mr. Hitchson said. He was visibly annoyed.
I laughed.

"No sir. Not at all. I find that a person's feelings toward God often shape how they feel about themselves."

"What do you mean?"

"I mean what I said."

MR. Hitchson shook his head.

"Can you give me an example?" He asked.

"Yes, sir I can. People who believe that God is coming to save them often play the role of the victim. They program into their subconscious that they need saving. As a result, they often find that they are not in control of their lives."

"I can kinda understand that, but I don't completely believe it."

"You believing it or not does not negate the fact that it's true."

"You know you have a very smart mouth. You need to watch it. Say the wrong thing to the wrong person and they might hurt you."

I smiled at him.

"I'm prepared to defend myself when I need to. I don't subscribe to the theology that God is a savior. I believe that God has given us the tools necessary to thrive in this life. Because of my belief; I am more than ready and willing to defend myself when necessary."

"Man, what kind of doctor are you? Mr. Hitchson said with a puzzled expression on his face."

"I'm a psychiatrist."

"What kind of doctor are you?" I asked.

"I'm not a doctor"

"What are you?"

"I'm a waiter at a restaurant."

"I thought you were a writer?"

"I am. But I've only sold ten books."

"Well Mr. Hitchson. How many did you sell last year?"

"None."

"Well you said more this year than you did last year. You've made progress. I'm proud of you keep up the good work." I said clapping my hands.

Mr. Hitchson didn't say anything.

"Back to your God complex; what sparked your search for a definition of God that was different from the one you were taught growing up."

Mr. Hitchson shook his head and smiled.

"You don't give up do you?"

"No sir. And neither should you. You have a lot of promise. You just have to realize it."

Mr. Hitchson blushed. Although he was dark brown; I could still tell that his face had turned red.

"I always had questions that no one would answer. Things that I was being taught didn't make sense to me.

"Like what" I asked. Walking towards my desk.

"Do you mind if I jot some things down while you talk?" I asked.

"No go right ahead." Mr. Hitchson said. He seemed uneasy.

I grab a legal pad and pen off my desk and return to my seat.

"You were saying?" I asked, "What didn't make sense to you?"

"The idea of heaven and hell."

"Ok I say. Will you please elaborate?"

"Let's say I've been a terrible person my entire life. Like I've committed every sin. I've hurt people. I've killed people, robbed them. Have had all the sex under the sun. Let's say someone comes to me with a gun and says they are about to kill me. Right before they pull the trigger; I confess my sins and ask God for his forgiveness. According to the Bible; I'll go to heaven. But on the flip side; let's say you have another person who has followed the bible to the letter. No sin. Always helping others. Goes to church faithfully and everything. Let's say that person hasn't eaten in four days, so they decide to steal some food.

Before they get to the store to steal the food; they get hit by

a car. Because they didn't repent for their sin. They go to

hell. That's crazy to me."

"I see your point." I say

I start doodling.

"And what about the people that have never heard

of Jesus or God? Do they automatically go to Hell?

"I'm glad you brought up Jesus." I say putting my

pad to the side. "I want your opinion on a theory I heard.

Jesus was not a messiah. Jesus was a freedom fighter. He

led a movement to free his people from the harsh treatment

they were experiencing at the hands of their oppressors. He

was captured, trialed, and killed publicly as a symbol of

what happens when black people attempt to help their

people. Judging the bible's account of his death; he was

essentially lynched. Like Nat Turner and countless other

black leaders. How does that make you feel?"

Mr. Hitchson was silent. He appeared to be speechless

"I know right. Take your time."

"I can see that being true." He finally said. "That actually makes more sense than what I've been taught. Where did you read that?"

I smiled.

"I didn't read it anywhere. I just made it up."

All the color left Mr. Hitchson's face. As if he had find something to believe in but immediately discovered it wasn't true.

"Why that face Mr. Hitchson?" I ask.

He shook his head.

"Because you're full of shit. I thought you knew what you were talking about, but you don't. You're full of shit."

"That's not nice Mr. Hitchson."

"You're not nice. Look how you've been talking to me. What kind of psychiatrist talks to his clients this way?"

"I may come off a little brash, but it's only because I don't sugar coat things. I must tell you the truth in a manner that you'll understand the importance of what I'm saying. You're not here for nice. You're not here for nice. You're here because your mind is all messed up and you need someone to help you un-mess it up."

Mr. Hitchson was silent again. I smiled. Placing my legal pad in front of me.

"So. Mr. Hitchson. What brings you in today?" I ask

He looked at me puzzled. I smiled at him.

"I came because I need advice, but you don't give advice."

"That's correct."

"So. What's the point?" HE said shrugging his shoulders.

"Great question Mr. Hitchson. That's where I've been leading you to this entire time."

I had resumed my doodling by this point.

"What's the point? Why are you here? Why were you born?"

"Is that a rhetorical question?"

"Not at all Mr. Hitchson."

"I was born because my dad's pull-out game was trash."

This caught me off guard; causing me to laugh loudly.

"There has to be a reason you were born though. That goes beyond your dad's weak pull out game."

"I don't know. I've never thought about it."

"That's surprising. I would think then when you were questioning the existence of God and trying to define them; you would have thought about your mortality. Interesting."

"What's interesting?"

"The fact that an intelligent non-believer of God hasn't thought about why he was born."

"I never said I didn't believe in God."

"Oh" I say looking up from my legal pad. "What did you say."

"I said I didn't know what I believed."

"So logically speaking it's possible that you believe that there is no God. Being that you said you don't know what you believe."

"No. That's not..."

"That wasn't a question."

"You said we would respect each other as a man, but you cut me off. That's not very respectful."

"You're right. I'll give you another free session."

"I don't want a free session.

"You want two free sessions?"

"No man. I don't want anything free from you."

I put my legal pad down.

"Mr. Hitchson, you can't afford to pay for a session with me. I charge $1,000 an hour during regular business hours. $3,000 for sessions after business hours. Looking at your watch and your car I know you can't afford me."

"There you go talking about my car and watch again."

I smiled.

"Well you were the one that introduced materialism into the conversation.

He was silent for a while. I continued to doodle.

"What are you writing?" he asked.

"I'm not writing anything. I'm doodling"

"What are you doodling?"

I show him the picture.

"Stick figures. You've been drawing stick figures this entire time."

"Not the entire time. I was playing tic tac toe initially. I don't know if I was more tired of losing to myself or beating myself." I say resuming my doodling.

Mr. Hitchson jumped from his seat.

"You haven't been listening. You've been too busy playing with your little picture" He shouted

"It is small isn't it?" I say shrugging. "At any rate. It's time for my next session. Meet with my assistant to schedule your next appointment."

"I'm not coming back. You suck as a psychiatrist" I was taken aback.

"Oh, do I" I say laughing. "I heard everything you said Mr. Hitchson. I could repeat it to you verbatim if you would like. I have perfect hearing, memory, and recall ability. Not to mention I record all sessions so if I can go back and listen just in case I feel I've missed something." Mr. Hitchson stood by the door with his back to me.

"But before you go; I must give you your final analysis."
Mr. Johnson turned to face me.

"I could tell something is troubling you. You seem to be lost. You have very little confidence in yourself. It is my suggestion that you find some things to like about yourself. Nothing like looks or materialistic items. Something inside of you. You'd really benefit from a knowledge of self-course. Before you return; do some research on Kemet. Get with Charlene to make your next appointment. Good day Mr. Hitchson.

"whatever"

He walked out the door.

Chapter 4: Debra Porter

"Mrs. Porter, how are you today," I ask.

"I'm ok," she says looking in my direction but not at me.

I could tell something was bothering her.

"Mrs. Porter we don't lie to one another.

She hesitated before speaking.

"I'm so got damn tired of black women being disrespected. Everyone disrespects us race by both genders. Hell, most of the disrespect comes from our own people," she yelled.

I remain silent. I have a feeling she isn't finished.

"It's ridiculous," she continued. "Enough is enough. No matter how hard we work, or try to play nice or try to follow the rules; we continued to be disregarded and disrespected."

She shook her head and mumbled something, but I couldn't hear what she said.

"Black women have been getting disrespected for centuries. You haven't expressed anything remotely mirroring your last statement. What triggered this new line of thought?"

"I read an article about the passenger that nearly died because the flight crew didn't believe the black woman was a doctor. Not to mention I was recently a victim of the gross disrespect we black women experienced in this raggedy ass state."

"I heard about the incident with the black woman on the plane. What happened with you?" I ask.
Mrs. Porter's eyes lit up.

"Isn't that crazy? I almost wish he died so his family could sue the crap out that airline. That's an easy case for ever the most mediocre attorney. That would teach them."
She looked at me.

"Is that wrong? That I'm willing to sacrifice that man's life to prove a point?" She asked.

"Yes. Very much so."
She shrugged.

"It's probably more wrong that I don't care that its wrong. Small sacrifice in the fight for black woman's respect. We've sacrificed for everyone else. It's time people sacrifice for us."

"People sacrificing or being scarified." I ask. "It's a huge difference."

"Whichever is the most beneficial. We sacrificed and were sacrificed for the so called good of society. So, I don't really give a damn about what others must do for us. As long as it gets done. Society owes us. Especially those sorry ass black men. All they want to do is have sex, play PlayStation, and eat. Waste of sperm and eggs.

Mrs. Porter was seething at this point. Clearly there was more bothering her than she was letting on. I made a mental note to revisit that subject, but first I would lead her to seeing how she contributed to the disrespect of her gender.

"What are willing to do to end the disrespect," I ask. "It seems like you are blaming everyone else, but not looking at your own behavior. Has it occurred to you that your actions may be not only hindering your progress but directly leading to your disrespect? You could be doing more to push forward your agenda."

"Like what black man. Please tell me which of my behaviors is causing you to disrespect me. While you're at it please tell me what I can do to help black women besides going to school and earning not one but two degrees. Besides mentoring young girls at the community center? And the tutoring and the other community service organizations I'm a part of. Tell me what else I should be doing. Don't you dare tell me I'm not doing my part."

I smiled. I had never seen her as worked up as she was. It was at that moment that I knew I had found a sore spot and I had to keep poking.

"I didn't say you weren't doing your part. I said you could be doing more.

"What more can I be doing? And with what time? I literally don't have time. After the partners work me nearly to death and the mentees finish the job I must find some life to give to my husband. I'm literally being the best black woman I can be."

"I hear what you're saying, but what if I said you aren't doing enough? What if I said your message isn't as effective as it could be? What if I told you that your physical appearance is negating all your efforts of helping those young girls.

Mrs. Porter looked at me with utter disdain. Like she couldn't believe what she was hearing. So, I continued.

"What if I said that in actuality; your physical appearance is doing far more damage than the good your service is doing?"

She was at a loss for words.

"What the hell are you talking about?" She finally said.

"Exactly what I said. You're causing those girls more harm than good." I said smiling.

"You're waiting for me to ask how aren't you?"

I shook my head.

"I'm not waiting per se. I know you're going to. It's more anticipating than waiting."

Mrs. Porter rolled her eyes.

"How is my appearance harming them," she asks.

"I'm glad you ask young lady. Here's how. It is my belief that confidence in oneself is the most important quality a person can possess. It is imperative that this confidence is developed while we are children. This is an extremely important pillar in a person's upbringing. A child must be confident not only in their intellectual, mental or emotional capabilities; they must be confident in all their capabilities; in all the areas that make up the human psyche. Do you agree with me so far?

"Yes," Mrs. Porter said reluctantly.

"Good. I can continue. Because you are a woman we will deal with the female psyche. Unfortunately, the dominant society places more emphasis on a woman's physical appearance than on any of her other attributes.

Doing so has caused many to believe that a woman's worth comes from how pleasing she is to the eye."

Mrs. Porter looked at me with her eye brows raised. This made me smile.

"Don't shoot the observer," I say. "But at any rate. To make things more troublesome for people of color; the dominant society Europeanized the standard of beauty. The closer a woman is to that standard the more beautiful she is considered similarly the farther away she is from that standard the less beautiful she is considered."

"Are we in agreeance that society is set up in this manner?"

She shook her head.

"Yes, but I don't see how you say I am harming black girls."

"We are getting there Mrs. Porter. Just go with me."

"Ok."

"Let's say we have a little black girl. For sake of this conversation we will call her Kennedy."

"Why Kennedy?"

"It's my daughter's name."

"I didn't know you had a daughter."

"I don't see why you would know that. Like I was saying; we have little girl Kennedy. Kennedy is old enough to have been victimized by the messages that white is beautiful and the farther you go away from white; the uglier you are. She is dealing with that on a psychological level that is greater than she can comprehend. She doesn't want to believe that she is ugly but what's considered beautiful doesn't look like her. Some way she can keep those thoughts at bay. She rationalizes that the only reason people that consider white to be more beautiful than white is white people. In her mind white people aren't the only beautiful people. Black people are beautiful too. She is holding on to this notion for dear life. One-day Kennedy runs into

Mrs. Debra Porter. 'Oh my God' she says. 'This woman looks like me and she is considered beautiful. I knew people that look like me could be beautiful too.'"

Mrs. Porter blushed.

"Upon further investigation; little Kennedy notices that the beautiful black woman is wearing fake hair. Hair that resembles that of a white woman. Kennedy is sad because her hair doesn't look like that. 'What else does she have that doesn't look like mine' Kennedy thinks. Little Kennedy sees that the pretty woman's eye lashes aren't real either. Kennedy panics. She stops looking at the pretty lady. She is confused. She didn't want to think that only white people were beautiful, but she sees that the beautiful black people are trying to look white. Kennedy doesn't look anything like this. She's the exact opposite. Subconsciously she arrives at the conclusion that if she is the exact opposite of the beautiful people she must be ugly. She begins hating the way she looks. She is convinced that she will never be accepted in a society that values her beauty more than any of her other attributes. Because she has no beauty; then she has no value. She now has low self-esteem. And is forced to search for acceptance and accept things that she's really too good for."

Mrs. Porter was speechless.

"All that because I have a weave and wear eye lashes."

"Yes. It's a slippery slope Mrs. Porter."

"But I don't wear weave because I have low self-esteem. I wear it because I need it."

"Why? Your hair doesn't grow?"

"It does, but it's bushy. I hate it."

"You hate the way your hair naturally grows out of your head, but you don't think you have low self-esteem."

"I don't. Wearing weave makes doing my hair in the mornings easier. My real hair doesn't suffer from damage because of the constant heat I'd have to apply to it.

Not to mention that fact that; nobody wears their real hair anymore."

"That's true. Nobody wears there anymore except for all the women that do."

"What black woman do you know that doesn't wear weave?"

"My wife. My mother. My assistant. My editor. The millions of women that have caused the boom in sales of products for natural hair. "

"Well I'm not them. I wear weave because I have to. Wearing my hair without weave isn't an option for me. It's too nappy. Too handle to manage. I would never climb the corporate ladder wearing my hair naturally. Black hair isn't desirable. My clients and the partners at my firm wouldn't stand for it. Plus natural hair is disgusting. Look at it," Debra said angrily.

I was genuinely confused. I didn't think I had heard her correctly.

"Excuse me Mrs. Porter, but I don't think I heard you correctly. Did you say that natural hair is disgusting?"

"Yes, that's what I said. Look at it. Ugh," she said shaking her head in disgust.

I smiled.

"So, you're saying the way that your hair natural grows out of your head is disgusting, but wearing someone or something else's hair isn't?"

"You make it sound worse than it is," She said.

I shake my head.

"Why are you shaking your head," she asked.

"Because I find it disturbing that women as intelligent as you are tricked into believing that something is wrong with their natural features. You all were tricked into believing that you were ugly by the same people selling you the products that are supposed to make you beautiful. It's one big hoax that you've fallen for. Not only have you fallen for it, but you perpetuate it consciously and subconsciously; you pass it down to your daughters and

nieces and cousins and little girls you don't even know.

They see you dismissing your natural features so guess

what? They do it also. You're directly responsible for

perpetuating the self-hate of the younger generation.

You're negatively impacting the very people you claim to

want to help, but that's not why we're here. How long

before you divorce your husband Mrs. Porter?"

Chapter 5: Debra Porter II

She was silent for a moment. I could tell she was caught off

guard by what I said.

"How did you know I'm about to divorce my

husband?" Mrs. Porter finally said.

"Because I know everything. During our last

session you stated that 'he doesn't fit in with your new

life'. In my experience when a woman says that she is

looking for a reason to leave her partner."

Mrs. Porter started crying.

"You must think I'm a terrible person."

"Yes, but not for the reasons you think."

"You should. I am a terrible person. I know how

hard he worked to pay for me to go to college and then to

law school. He did that for me. Worked double and triple

shifts. I know he hated that, but he wanted me to be happy.

I said I wouldn't be happy unless I was lawyer. He helped

make that possible."

Mrs. Porter continued to sob. I'm accustomed to my clients crying, but not like this. I have never heard anyone cry as hard as she was crying.

"If you know he did all that for you; why are you trying to leave him," I asked.

"Because he doesn't fit in. He's not impressionable. He doesn't know how to work a room. He's not real charming. The partners at my firm and my colleagues have all said the same thing. They said he doesn't fit in. They say they don't see why I'm with him. He's holding me back."

Mrs. Porter had her head in her hands.

"Isn't most of the partners at your firm white?"

She started sniffling.

"Yes. So? What does that mean?"

"Have you considered he doesn't fit in because he's a hardworking blue collar black man?"

She looked at me like she didn't know what I was getting at. So, I continued.

"Your colleagues and your husband operate in two totally different worlds. It's not your husband's job to appease your colleagues or any of the people are you trying to rub shoulders with. He doesn't have to be around those people. There's a very good chance that he doesn't desire to be around them. Doesn't enjoy their company. Based on what you've told me; it's not hard to imagine him unintentionally sulking during an event.

"He does," she yelled excitedly.

"Your colleagues have undoubtedly noticed his disdain."

"Yes, they have. They've joked about it around the office. Several times in fact. They call him Mr. Too Good. They say he thinks he's too good for them."

"They may be true. Corporate people tend to be some of the vilest most disloyal people on the planet. Especially lawyers. You're starting to fit in perfectly"

Mrs. Porter looked offended.

"But I'm a corporate lawyer and I'm not vile. I don't fit into that category."
I smiled.

"You sure? We've discussed how you're poisoning the minds of young black girls while disguising it as community service and you're plotting to leave your husband, the man that sacrificed so that your dreams could be realized. You don't think those are the actions of a vile person? You're exploiting young black girls and casted aside a black man after you no longer need him. In essence you're a white feminist."

Mrs. Porter looked stunned.

"I'm not going to allow you to diminish the work I do with those young girls. I put my heart and sold into my community service projects. I'm providing them with a strong black mentor. Someone that has achieved success. And looks like them. And you're not going to make me feel worse than I do about my husband,"
Mrs. Porter was expressing a mixture of sadness, anger, and embarrassment. I could tell she was still processing what I said about her volunteer work, but she couldn't give that her full attention. She felt deep sorrow for her husband. She loved him, but no longer saw a future with him.

"Do you really look like them though? Or do you look like what society tells them they have to look like in order to be accepted? The question you must ask yourself is 'are you a beacon of hope or are you confirmation of their ideas that they're natural appearance will not allow them to be successful in life. Another thing we must discuss is who defines success? Why do we allow people to define success for us, but that's a conversation for a different day. Back to what's most important; you abandoning your husband. How are you going to tell him," I asked.

Mrs. Porter looks at me while she processes everything I had just said. She didn't appear to have the energy to engage me on my idea of her being a bad role model.

"I don't know how I'm going to tell him or when I'm going to tell him. I honestly don't have all the answers to the questions he's going to have. I don't know," She said finally.

She looked at me. She wanted me to tell her how she should it. I wouldn't. Not because I didn't have any suggestions, but because she needed to figure it out on her own. She knew more about him than I did. She alone would know the best way to break the news. When she realized I wouldn't give her any suggestions. She began sobbing into her hands. I allowed her to cry.

"It's not like I don't love him," she said in between bouts of sob. "I do love him. I want to be married. I want to still be in love with him."

"You saying still be in love with him is misleading. It makes it seem that you were at one point in love with him. We both know that that's not the case."
She looked at me.

"You don't know what the hell you're talking about. I was in love with him. Deeply in love."
She paused.

"I mean he just doesn't excite me anymore. I'm not excited to see him walk through the door. I'm not excited to hear how his day was. I don't know what it is."
She resumed crying.

"You need to admit to yourself and him that you were never in love with him."

"Why do you keep saying that? It's not true. You're trying to get in my head and make me thing I'm a bad person. That's not true. I used to be in love with him. He used to excite me. I used to get excited at the very thought of him. It's gone. My excitement for him is gone. Oh God what's wrong with me?" she said before sobbing.

"I have a theory. I developed it during our last session, but we ran out of time before I could express it."

"Of course, you have a theory. You have a theory for everything. You should change your name to theory this. Theory that. Maybe I don't want to hear your theory. Have you thought of that? No of course you haven't. You're too busy thinking of theories. You don't consider that people don't want to hear them. 'I have a theory' Take your theory to the bank and try to cash it. Ass."

It was difficult to understand what she was saying. It was a mixture of crying and talking. I hate when people do that. She reminded me of the prostitute from Sprung. She looked at me as if she was waiting for something.

"What," I finally say.

"You said you had a theory. What is it?"

"My theory is that you never were in love with him. You were in love with the way he treated you and his willingness to assist you in getting to where you wanted to be. You used him to get ahead in life and now that he's no longer useful; you are tossing him aside."

"That's asinine," Mrs. Porter said.
She clearly was outraged by my theory.

"Of course I was in love with him," she continued. "I wouldn't have married him if I wasn't. I'm not tossing him aside. I deserve to be with someone that excites me. I want to be excited. Staying with him knowing the way I feel is wrong. I'll only be hurting us. Are you calling me a gold digger?"

"Oh really," I say smiling. "I'm not calling you a gold digger in the sense that you're after materialist things, but one can easily make the case that you're a goal digger. I'll show you how I arrived at my conclusion. During our last session you told me that one of things you admired

most about him is that he never allowed you to pay for

things.”

"Yes, that's true. He still does that even though I

make twice as much as he does.”

"Because money isn't important to him. The ability

to provide is more important. It's safe to say that prior to

him; you had never dated anyone that did.”

"Yes. Before him I always had to pay on dates.

There are a lot of bums out there.”

"You're about to date a lot more bums after you get

this divorce, but that's not what we are talking about. We

are talking about you never being in love with your

husband and you being a goal digger.”

Mrs. Porter stared at me as if she wanted to say something,

but didn't know what to say. So, she said nothing.

"By paying for everything; he gave you a feeling

you'd never had before. He was providing for you.

Because you had never experienced a man providing for you; you didn't know how to properly process those emotions."

"How do you know my father wasn't in my life," She asked.

"I can tell by the way you carry yourself. As I was saying; your inability to properly process those emotions caused you think that you loved him. You began doing all the things you knew to do that would cause him to reciprocate that love. That led him to think that you were the one. So he proposed. Being that you two were involved intimately; he was aware of your dream to be a lawyer. As a provider he knew he would have to make that dream a reality. So he sent you to law school."

Mrs. Porter was looking out the window at this point. I smiled.

"While in law school," I continued. "You were the most affectionate towards him. He could do no wrong. He was your everything. Here was your husband providing

you the opportunity to live out your dream as a lawyer.

You're still unable to properly process your emotions so

you think you're, for lack of a better word, super in love.

Am I right?"

Mrs. Porter didn't say anything. She continued to look out

the window. I knew she was thinking about what I was

saying.

"But the problem came after you graduated, found a

job, and started climbing the ladder."

She finally looked at me.

"Welcome back," I say.

She rolled her eyes. I smiled.

"Now that you're climbing the ladder," I continued.

"You need him to provide like he used to. You're being

told that a more personable husband would help you climb

the ladder faster. A husband that thrives at dinner parties is

more beneficial. Your current husband isn't that person.

You're aware of this; so what do you do? You divorce him and find someone that can help you achieve your goal. Hence the term goal digger. It's not entirely your fault. The fact that you didn't have both parents in your life while you were growing up crippled you emotionally. You weren't able to witness the complete range of emotions that male and female's experience.   Your lack of emotional education set you down a dark path. Most people don't even know that they are emotionally retarded. They lack an emotional balance. They deal with situations one of two ways. Both are extreme. In life there needs to be a balance. Most people don't have that balance. That's not healthy."

I looked at Mrs. Porter just as she resumed sobbing heavily. I watched. I thought about continuing to expound on my theory, but I decided against it. She had heard enough for this session. I glanced at my watch. It was almost lunch time.

"Mrs. Porter," I say. "What are you eating for lunch?"

She looked at me through teary eyes.

"I have a lunch date with some of my coworkers."

"Where are you going?"

"Nostalgia. I hear their food is really good."

"It is. I plan to go there also."

She didn't say anything.

"Well that concludes today's sessions. Don't forget to get with Charlie before you leave."

We stood up simultaneously. I walked her to the door.

"Have a good day Mrs. Porter. I will see you next week."

She smiled and walked out the door.

Chapter 5: Harry Davis

I come out my office to see Debbie talking to my friend Harry. I shake my head. Judging by the look on her face; she's obviously enthralled by his charm. I continue to shake my head. I know how this will play out. Based on her mental state; bedding her will almost be too easy.

Right now, her guard is down because Harry appears to be harmless. He will give her his number.

Allowing her to feel as though she is in control, however that is far from the truth. Once she contacts him he will invite her to an event. Some type of exclusive soiree; with the goal to be to make her feel like she is important. He will show her off and make her feel like she's the center of his universe. He will pull away suddenly and unexplainably. Doing so will create confusion in her mind. After she reaches out to him he will tell her something about not being able to focus when he's around her and how he wants her so desperately, but doesn't want her to feel like he's only after her for the sex. At this point all her defenses are down and he will swoop in for the kill. They will have sex a few times and things will appear to be going perfectly but then he will pull away again. This time permanently. I've seen it so many times.

Right on schedule Ms. Dotson pulls out her phone to get his contact information. They shake hands and she leaves.

"What did I tell you about flirting with my clients,"

I say walking towards him.

He looked at me smiled.

"You saw that? I was trying to be finished before

you walked out."

We shake hands.

"I couldn't help myself." He continued. "Look at

her. That chocolate skin and those dimples. I don't usually

like weave, but her booty makes up for it."

I laugh.

"You're an animal." I say.

Harry has been my friend since we were kids. We

grew up in the same neighborhood, The New projects. Our

friendship started out rocky. We wanted the same girl. Her

name was Alicia Smith. We both thought we were the first

in line to be her boyfriend. We both wined and dined her

best a 10-year-old kid could. She played us against one

another. We were on the verge of fighting until we saw her kiss another boy. We've been friends ever since.

Harry and I are more than just best friends. We are business partners. We own the publishing company that publishes my books, a couple dozen rental properties, and even the building our offices are in. He loaned me the money to keep me afloat when I started my own practice. I did the same for him.

"What do you want for lunch," He asks tearing me away from my daydream.

I think for a moment.

"Nostalgia"

"Of course, that's what you want," Harry says

"If you knew; why'd you ask?"

"I honestly don't know."

I go to Nostalgia for lunch at least three times a week. The food is amazing, but the atmosphere is what I like the most. The owner is black, ex- football player. It's usually filled with professional black people. Something about black

people and vegetarian food entices me. I shrug my

shoulders.

"What can I say? I love their food."

"I know. Best rabbit food in town," He says

mocking me.

We both laugh.

"I'll be gone for about an hour. If Mr. Johnson

arrives before I return; let him in my office. Text me if you

need me," I say to Charlie.

She smiles.

"Let me see your phone." She says

"Why" I ask handing it to her.

"Because I need to make sure it's not on silent, so

you'll know when I call you.

My phone is always on silent. I don't like feeling like I'm

a slave to it. Like everything it goes off I must check it. So,

I leave it silent and check it whenever I'm ready to.

"Yes mam," I say placing my phone back in my pocket.

Nostalgia is within walking distance from our building. I enjoy the walk. It allows me to think and watch people; two of my favorite hobbies.

"I have an idea for one of the vacant offices." Harry said

"I'm listening."

"We are going to turn it into surgical offices and make them available for traveling doctors."

"How much is that going to cost?"

"Are you asking because you want to know or because you feel you're supposed to?"

"Because I'm supposed to."

Harry laughs.

"You rich people and your lack of concern about how your money is being spent make me sick."

I didn't say anything.

"What do you think?"

"About what," I ask.

"About my idea."

"It's a good idea. You have my full support."
We arrive at Nostalgia in no time. It's lunch time so the owner will be there. I never found out why he chose Mondays to be there. If I had to guess it's because it's the first day of the week and he wants to start off the week right, however I don't know for certain. I thought about asking, but never got around to it.

"Welcome to Nostalgia," He says.
He's a giant of a man. If I had to guess, I'd say he was at least seven feet tall.

"Hey," He says more enthusiastically when he recognizes us. "Dr. Jenkins. Mr. Davis. It's so nice to see you two.

He greets us like this every time he sees us. Like he hasn't seen us in years.

"Greetings sir", I say shaking his hand.
He shakes it eagerly. He does the same with Harry's.

"There is a wait time of about five minutes. I apologize, but we are packed."

"We are ok with waiting." Harry says.
We take a seat and await an available table. The wait allows me to people watch. It's not long before I see something interesting.

A couple are walking out of the restaurant. They appear to be at odds with one another. He's walking in front of her with a frown on his face. She's staring at the back of head like she's contemplating how much time she would get for murder.

"I know her." Harry leans over and whispers to me. The man turns and faces her just as she sees Harry. Her face lights up.

"Hey" she says.

Harry smiles and waves.

"Are you screwing him too?" The man yells.
A combination of horror, guilt, and embarrassment spread
cross the woman's face. She quickly snaps out of it.

"Oh my God. You're so insecure. You think I'm
screwing everyman with a penis."

"Because you are." The man yells.

"Well Albert if you could last longer than ninety
seconds I wouldn't need to cheat, now would I?"
They exit the restaurant still yelling at one another. I look
to Harry for answers. He was shaking his head.

"He really is insecure." He says

"So, you didn't sleep with her."
Harry smiled.

"Look at her," Harry says seriously. "Of course, I
did. A few days ago actually."
I laugh.

"So, his insecurity is somewhat founded in truth.

"Yes somewhat. She's not sleeping with every guy
she knows. Just me."

"You think you're the only one," I ask.

"I better be. I told her that I found out there was
someone else I would call her husband and let him know
she's cheating on us."
We both laughed. Even the woman next to us laughed.

"You're wrong for that," She said continuing to
laugh.

"I'm just saying. At least I told her the truth."
The lady shook her head and continued to laugh.

"Dr. Jenkins. Mr. Davis your table is ready."
We follow the owner to our table.

"Your waitress will be with you shortly." He said
placing the menus on the table. "I apologize for that couple
arguing. We don't condone that sort of behavior here."

"It's ok. We don't fault you for that."

"Ok. Enjoy your meal gentlemen."

I look at Harry.

"Why are you looking at me?" He asked.

"Because I don't understand how you're so pro black, but won't commit to one black woman and you sleep with married black women."

Harry smiles and leans forward.

"It's quite simple sir. I am a whore. I come from a long line of whores. My daddy was a whore. My daddy's daddy was a whore. I didn't choose this whoredom. This whoredom chose me."

I laugh

"Or are you really a white supremacist?"

"What?" He said confused

"Think about it. You are continuously hurting black women; both mentally and emotionally. They misconstrue your whoredom with a sense that they are inadequate. This causes their self-esteem to be negatively affected. They began to lose the capacity to have healthy relationships with other men. Especially black men. So now, women that would marry good black men and raise strong intelligent black children; marry white men or cease dating men period. In essence you're contributing to the destruction of the black race. And because you only date black women; women of other races are spared your destructive behavior. You're a black white supremist. I'm really disgusted with you."

I shake my head to drive my point home. Harry stared at me a long moment before exploding with laughter.

"As much as I hate to admit it; you're actually right."

Harry shook his head. He was smiling hard.

"Welcome to Nostalgia. My name is Ebony, and I'll be your waitress. May I start with your drink order?"

"Wow a white girl named Ebony," I say.

She blushed.

"I get that a lot," She said.

"Well white Ebony. My name is Harry Davis and I just found out I am a black white supremacist.

"What." Ebony asked confused.

"Don't mind him," I interjected. He's off his meds. I'll have water with lemon and honey."

"Yes sir." She said. "And for the black white supremacist."

We all laughed.

"Touché' young lady." Randy said smiling. "I'll have water with lemon also, but with no ice. I'm allergic." I shook my head. It took a moment for Ebony to process what Harry said.

"What" She finally said.

Harry laughed. She looked at me for clarification.

"Don't worry about it young lady," I said shaking my head.

"Ok?" She said before walking away.

"Why do you always bother the waitress when we're here?"

Harry smiled.

"I told you earlier. I'm going to ask her what she's doing for the black lives matter movement." He says.

"Why would you do that?" I ask puzzled.

"You say why I say why not?" Harry said still smiling.

I shake my head.

"But seriously. I forgot to tell you what I did the other day." Harry says.

"What happened?"

"So I was at the mall trying on suits."

"You were at the mall trying out suits? Not you Mr. I Only Wear Tailored Suits."

"I know right, but I was with Ashley. Remember her?"

"The teacher with the big forehead, brown eyes and that drove that old red car?" I asked.

"Yes her."

"No I don't remember her."

Harry laughed.

"You really are an asshole."

At the moment. Ebony returned with our drinks.

"Here you go gentlemen." She said placing the drinks in front of us. "Do you know what you'll be having?"

"Yes we are ready." Harry said. "I'll have the fish and grits. Extra Crawfish butter on the side. I have a question."

"Yes sir?"

"What are you doing for the black lives matter movement?" Harry asked.

Harry's question took Ebony by surprise. She looked at me for clarification. I shrugged my shoulders.

"What do you mean?" Ebony said. She was clearly uncomfortable.

"I mean exactly what I said young lady. How are you contributing to the black lives matter movement?"

"I haven't contributed anything." Ebony said nervously.

"Why haven't you?" Ebony appeared to be at a loss for words. She didn't know what to say. Even if she knew what to say; I don't think she knew how to say it.

"I didn't know I was supposed to," she said finally.

"Of course you are young lady. Everyone that benefits or enjoys black culture is required to assist us in our fight for equality. You have cornrows, work in a black owned establishment and undoubtedly listen to Rap music. You have a duty to help my people. You can't emulate us and turn a blind eye to our suffering. Plus your name is Ebony."

I completely agreed with Harry. Judging by the look on

Ebony's face; she agreed also.

"You're right. What can I do to help?" she asked.

"Beats me Ebony. I was asking you in hopes that

you could tell me what to do." Harry said smiling broadly.

Ebony didn't know what to say or what to do. She just

stood there in awe. She eventually regained her composure.

She looked at me.

"Can I have your food order?

"I'll have the vegetarian lasagna with corn and

asparagus."

Ebony smiled.

"Good choice," She said. "I'll get these in for you."

"Thank you." I said.

Ebony walked away. She looked back towards our table

and shook her head.

"Like I was saying," Harry said. "I was in the

dressing room. I had just taken off my clothes and the urge to piss hit me all of a sudden. The bathroom was on the other end of the store. I knew I wouldn't make it."

I shook my head. I had a feeling I knew where this was going.

"So I piss in the corner of the dressing room."

"What." I said laughing and confused at the same time.

"Yep right there in the corner. My sock got wet. I was so mad."

I continued laughing. Harry was laughing too.

"Why are you so nasty?" I asked.

"I'm not nasty."

"Lies." I say loudly. "How many times have you sat in your car and pissed in a cup because you couldn't make it to the bathroom?"

"I plead the fifth."

I shook my head.

"Didn't you piss in Ashley's garbage can?" I asked.

Harry laughed loudly.

"You're nasty bruh."

Harry and I laughed loudly. Lunch continued the same way it started. Me lecturing Harry and him flirting with the waitress.

"I'm thinking about investing money in one of my patients." I said was we entered the building.

"Why?" Harry asked.

"He has potential. He reminds me a lot of us."

"How so?"

"He's black."

Harry laughed.

"What does he do?"

"He's a writer." I say as we enter the elevator.

Harry laughed again.

"Why are you laughing."

"Because he's trying to be a writer."

"Would you have laughed if I had said he's trying to be a rapper?"

"No. How are you going to help? Are you going to sign him to the publishing company"?

"No. He started his own publishing company. I'm going to introduce him to Cheryl and get him a distribution deal.

"Sounds good."

I step I'm off the elevator.

"I'm glad you think so. Let me know when you call Cheryl and set up the deal." I say as the elevator closes.

Chapter 7: Rodney Johnson

When I walked into the foyer; Charlie informed me that Rodney Johnson was in my office waiting on me. I've seen Mr. Johnson twice before. He was referred by Harry. Mr. Johnson really enjoys drinking. Maybe a little too much for normal society, however according to Harry; he's extremely successful. He owns several body shops and is a silent partner at his brother's Engineering firm.

"Good afternoon Mr. Johnson," I say as I walk into my office.

"Hey doctor," he said without looking at me. "I hope you don't mind; I've helped myself to a drink."

"No, I don't mind at all."

"Good. This is my second one." Mr. Johnson said smiling at me.

I smiled too taking my suit jacket off and hanging it up. I grabbed a pen and legal pad and headed to my chair. Mr. Johnson was already sitting. He had on his work uniform. I didn't understand why he wears it. He didn't actually work on any vehicles.

"Mr. Johnson I've meaning to ask you; why do you wear a mechanic's jump suit?"

"That's really quite simple," Mr. Johnson said. "I'm a mechanic."

"Technically, but you don't repair any vehicles."

"Of course not, but if I need to I will."

"So you wear that just in case you have to get under the hood."

Mr. Johnson laughed.

"No. If I have to get under the hood of a car someone is getting fired."

I still didn't understand. He was intentionally dodging my question.

"So why wear it," I asked.

Mr. Johnson took a very large gulp.

"Because it pisses people off. Especially you well to do black people and those racist white bastards. They see me at their fancy restaurants wearing a dirty uniform, but they can't say anything to me because I have more money than most of them. Don't get me wrong I can throw on a monkey suit and look 'presentable', but I won't because I don't care what you think of me. I'm going to drink my whiskey, ride in my old beat up tuck, and continue to cash all these checks."

I had to admit that I understood where he was coming. I washed Mr. Johnson take another large gulp of his drink.

"That's 12-year-old cognac you've been gulping down," I say. "I'm told you're supposed to sip it slowly. So you'll enjoy all the flavors."

"12 years old. I thought it tasted a little funny. This is spoiled. I can't have you offering spoiled alcohol to your clients. I'm going to have to drink the rest of it so can you buy some fresh liquor."

Mr. Johnson was smiling broadly. I sniggled a little at his joke.

"How's everything today Mr. Johnson." I ask.

"Everything is fine. Life is perfect. Happening the way it's supposed to.

"Good. How's your son. Demond."

Mr. Johnson shook his head.

"Let me tell you what he and his little nigga kid friends did."

I chuckled at little nigga kid friends.

"I'm listening," I say. Still chuckling.

"So some new tennis shoes came out last weekend. Demond asked me for some money to buy him. He told me they are $200. No way in hell I'm spending $200 on tennis shoes."

Mr. Johnson took a sip of his drink. It was more of a gulp.

"It's a shame you don't drink doc. This shit is really smooth."

"IT should be. It's $2000 a bottle." I said as he was taking another large sip

Mr. Johnson choked.

"What the hell Doc." He said in between coughing. "You spent $2000 on liquor that you don't even drink? You're a fool. A rich educated one at that."

I didn't know if I was supposed to be offended by his comment, so I didn't say thank you.

"How did you find this? Did you go to the liquor store and ask for the most expensive bottle they had?" Mr. Johnson asked.

I smiled.

"No." I say. "My business partner."

"Are you talking about Harry?"

"Yes. Harry"

"Just say is name. You people kill me with that. Saying things to make you seem more important. His name is Harry. I know his name. Just say his name."

I smile

"My apologies Mr. Johnson. I forgot you knew him. Harry told me it was a good choice, so I purchased it. How much do you spend on your liquor?"

"Me." Mr. Johnson said in between sips. "Shit I'm good with a $25 fifth of gentleman Jack. And when I'm feeling saddity I'll get a $40 bottle of VSOP."

"Oh I say."

"I'm about to stop drinking though."

"Any particular reason?" I ask.

"Yes I want to see how successful I can be if I'm

sober. I think I can be a lot more successful. So I'm about

to test my theory."

"That's interesting."

"What is?" He asked.

"You know that if you didn't drink as much; you'd

be more successful. You're aware that alcohol is hindering

your mobility in life. Most alcoholics don't admit that

while they're intoxicated."

"I'm far from drunk Doc and I'm offended that you

call me an alcoholic." Mr. Johnson said smiling. "I'm not

an alcoholic. I'm a drunk. Alcoholics go to meetings. Us

drunks just like to drink."

I couldn't help but laugh at his joke.

"Well you've admitted that alcoholic is holding you

back in life. What are you going to do about it?"

Mr. Johnson shook his head.

"I just told you I'm about to stop drinking. Got damn Doc you don't listen. All this money for a session and you don't listen? You didn't even ask 'how does that make you feel' like they do on TV. I can do what you do?" I smiled.

"You're not the first of my clients to say that to me today. It seems that everyone thinks they can be a psychiatrist."

"Doc I know a dude that is better at this than you. Give him a pint of whiskey and he'll solve all your problems."

"Maybe I should give him a job."

"Naw. You don't want him around all your fancy clients. He smells bad and I'm sure he steals."

I didn't know what to say. So I said nothing.

Mr. Johnson got up and fixed himself another drink.

"I thought you were about to stop drinking." I say.

"I am. One day. But not today. I told you I have to help you get rid of all this spoiled liquor."

I smiled and shook my head; watching him pour his drink. I've always marveled at how some raging alcoholics could be extremely successful and happy. Honestly part of me was envious of him. He could indulge in his vice of choice and still function. Marijuana and I never could figure out how to do that.

"What were we talking about," he said returning to his seat.

"We were talking about you no longer drinking and your son asking for $200 to buy some tennis shoes."

"Oh yeah," He said before taking a large sip. "So after I told him no. He asked if he could earn the money. I told him I had room for him in one of my shops or he could help clean a one of the buildings. He didn't like any of those suggestions. He said he'd figure something out. Mind you this conversation was Wednesday.

Mr. Johnson paused to take another sip.

"Fast forward to Saturday afternoon he and his little nigga kid friends came into the house with bags from the mall. All of them smiling and having a jolly ole time. Demond comes into the living room where I'm having my usual afternoon drink and shows me the shoes. I must admit. I like them, but I know I didn't give him the money for them, so I needed answers.

Mr. Johnson started laughing.

"This boy and his little nigga kid friends came up with a scheme and scammed the white folks in the neighborhood." Mr. Johnson said before resuming his laughing.

I was confused.

"What do you mean?"

Mr. Johnson continued to laugh.

"I mean him and his little nigga kid friends went door to door asking for donations for their basketball team.

Mr. Johnson exploded in laughter. I didn't see what was funny about the deceptive behavior. He could tell I wasn't in on the joke.

"Why are you looking at me like that" he asked.

"I don't find their actions funny. They preyed on the charity of innocent people."

"Hold up Doc. The while folks in my neighborhood are a lot of things, but innocent ain't one of them. He's the thing about Demond. He's a terrible basketball player. He's a nerd. That's why I'm laughing so hard."
I still didn't understand.

"So why lie about basketball. Why not do a fundraiser for activities that he's actually apart of?"

"I asked him the same thing. Why not mention The National Honor's society or Chess Club or Science Club? He said he did at first, but he wasn't receiving any donations. It's like the white folks didn't believe that a black kid was a member of those organizations, so he switched it up and said basketball."

Mr. Johnson fell into a fit of laughter and nearly spilled his drink.

"Hold up," he said sitting up straight. "Let me get myself together. I don't believe in spilling alcohol." He took the final sip of his drink. I never understood how people could drink alcohol. It's literally poison, but I never believed in judging anyone. I went to medical school not law school.

"Why is this so funny to you," I asked. "I don't see how you as a business man could condone such manipulative business practices. I would be outraged."

"I was at first doc, but when he told me that they didn't believe he was smart; I was angry. White folks thinking my son aren't smart because he's black. He used their racist beliefs to his advantage and outsmarted them. To hell with them."

Mr. Johnson shook his head.

"But I did make him take the shoes back. And give the money to one of mamas that were in the store. Then I bought him the shoes."

"That was kind of you." I say

"Well Doc I'm a kind person. Contrary to popular belief. Can you belief those racist bastards had a petition going around to have us kicked out the neighborhood." Mr. Johnson said looking at me.

"After they found out they were lied to; I don't blame them."

"They didn't find out. This was when we first moved in. They had a problem with a big black man living in their neighborhood. Then when word got out that I bought my house right out. They sho nuff wanted me out. They kept reporting me to the police. Saying I was a drug dealer and all manner of things. But what really angered me is that the very people that started the petition were the ones that smiled at me and spoke to me all the time. I hate fake people. IF you don't like me don't like me, but don't be fake about it."

"I understand. I don't like that either. Well actually I don't really care. I don't care about people though honestly. House already paid off; that's impressive. Harry said you were successful, but clearly he downplayed it."

"I wish Harry would stop telling people my damn business." Mr. Johnson said getting up to fix himself another drink."

I didn't say anything.

"I am successful, but it's nothing compared to how much success I'd have if I wasn't addicted to alcohol, but that's a horse of another color. I don't like owing people anything. Especially white folks. If you miss a payment; they'll come, take your shit. I don't have time for that."

"You really hate white people I see."

"And you must really love them? Uncle Tom taking up for them."

I smiled.

"I've been called that before by some angry black people but that's far from the truth. I don't take up for white people; I just want black people to take more responsibility for their actions. We all know about the atrocities committed by white people, but what is harboring on them going to do for our community? I'll tell you what; nothing."

"You have a point. But no I don't hate white people. Only white men. I love white women."

"What caused your hatred?"

Mr. Johnson laughed.

"Ah shit now. Is this when you try to get in my head and make me and cry and all of that other stuff." He said.

"Something like that" I said. "I'm actually intrigued by you"

He looked at me with confusion.

"Whoa Doc. You seem like a nice guy, but I don't like you like that. I'm not judging you or anything, you've clearly spent too much time around white folks, but I don't swing that way."

It took a moment for me to realize what he was saying.

"No," I exclaimed. "You have the wrong idea. I'm not gay."

"Sure you're not," he said with a smirk on his face. "Again Doc I'm not judging. Do you. Just stay over there with that."

"I have a wife and a daughter."

"Oh so you're one of those undercover brothers. On the down low. It's you gays that I don't like. You're posing as a heterosexual male while all the while hiding your bag in somebody's husband's rear compartment."

Mr. Johnson shook his head. I didn't bother responding. I knew there was no winning this battle. I've never been good at playing the dozens. I was a little distraught. Mr.

Johnson saw my facial expression and erupted in laughter.

"I'm just talking shit buddy," he said.

I exhaled.

"Back to your question. When I was a teenager I

was beat up by a group of white men. I've hated them

every since. A few months after that I got head from a

white girl. I've loved them ever since."

I chuckled.

"That's perfectly understandable." I say

"What about you Doc. How many white nappy

dugouts have you gone camping in?"

I laughed again.

"None actually. I've only dated black women."

"That's surprising. I just knew you had some white

Nubian queens under your belt. Harry is the same way. I

told him he doesn't know what he's missing. Nothing like

enduring a racist white man during the day and taking your anger out on some white poom poom."

"You don't feel any shame sleeping with white women? Our ancestors were killed just for looking at them."

"Exactly," he said excitedly. "I'm doing this for them. For all the times they had to say, 'yes Ms. Annie' I make a white woman beg to touch me. For every rape, beating, and verbal assault; I'm tearing through another piece of white flesh. I'm really a black activist. I should get a metal or something like that."

Mr. Johnson took a sip of his drink. I couldn't argue with his logic. I've had numerous clients express his sentiment. Having sex with white women is their way of getting back at white men.

"I'm guessing your son is mixed."

"No of course not. He's 100% black. His mama is as black as they come. Well she was. She died six years ago."

"Sorry to hear that."

"It's cool. I'm passed it now."

"We never truly get passed the death of a loved one. Especially in this society. How Does Demond feel about you dating again? Specifically, white women.

"I don't bring women around him. Especially white ones. He's had a tough enough time dealing with his mama's death. I don't want to cause any additional grieve by bringing women around before he's ready. I told him I'd wait until he's ready or go off to college."

"That's admirable."

Mr. Johnson looked at me.

"No Doc. I'm admirable.

Chapter 8: Rodney Johnson II

I sit and watch Mr. Johnson enjoy his drink. It's a tactic I like to use. Allow my patients to sit in silence. Allowing them to think to themselves. Eventually they'll bring up a subject they want to talk about. That works for most patients; however Mr. Johnson isn't one of them. If I was a gambling man; I would bet money that if I didn't initiate

conversation, he wouldn't say anything. He'd just sit there

and enjoy his drink. I'm tempted to test my theory;

however doing so doesn't serve either of us well.

"How do you feel about bullying Mr. Johnson?" I

ask.

"What do you mean," he asks with a look of

confused look on his face.

"Bullying," I say slower making sure to pronounce

all the letters. "How do you feel about it?"

"I heard what you said. I just don't know what

you're talking about or why you're talking about it."

"I explain a little bit why I brought it up. You don't

know what bullying is?"

Mr. Johnson looked at me.

"Of course I know what it is. Why did you bring it

up now? Am I bullying you?" Mr. Johnson said taking a sip

of his drink. "I'm just about out." He said looking at his glass.

He clearly was trying to decide if he would make another. The container was nearly empty. I had never seen anyone be able to consume so much alcohol in such a little time. He still seems relatively normal. It's amazing.

"I'll have Charlie get another bottle of that, but in the meantime I have more liquor in the cabinet. You can continue to help yourself." I say.

"You don't have to tell me twice." Mr. Johnson said jumping to his feet. "I appreciate you Doc. No one I know will buy $2000 liquor. And they certainly wouldn't let me drink it at will. You're a class act Doc."

"I don't know what to say. Thank you I guess. My former mentor use to say 'alcohol is meant to be drank not sit in a pretty glass to look all pretty'"

"He's a wise man Doc. I don't care what they say about you you're ok with me."

"Thank you Mr. Johnson," I say watching him feel his glass to the rim. "The reason I mentioned bullying is because of a video I watched a few days ago."

"Oh you're talking about the little with boy," Mr. Johnson said returning to his seat. He was obviously pleased with himself for not spilling any. "This will be my last one."

I smile.

"Of course it will. The container is empty."

"You told me to help myself." Mr. Johnson said smiling. "And I told you I was going to have to finish it. I couldn't in good conscious allow you to serve spoiled liquor. Especially not cognac. I'm really looking out for you. You really should offer me a free session or something."

Mr. Johnson couldn't contain his laughter. I just shook my head. I always enjoyed drunkard banter.

"What were you saying about the little white boy in the video?"

"In the video I'm referencing; it was a black man referencing the white child. He was talking about how black athletes and entertainers quickly galvanized behind the young white kid, but haven't didn't mention anything about the two black girls that committed suicide because of the same reason."

Mr. Johnson shook his head. I was eager to hear what he was going to say.

"You want to use the last few minutes of my session to discuss how black people don't support each other," he said.

Mr. Johnson laughed. I just looked at him. Undoubtedly he had experience with black people not supporting him. I wanted to divide deeper into that, however this wasn't the session to do so. I made a mental not to revisit that subject during our next session, but for now I must stay the course.

"Not quite," I say. "I want to discuss causes and effects."

"How did you get that from bullying?"

"It's really quite simple Mr. Johnson. You see there are usually two victims in incidents of bullying. The victim of bullying and the actually bully."

Mr. Johnson looked perplexed, but didn't say anything. He continued to drink from his glass. I waited again to see if he would add anything. He didn't say I continued.

"Allow me to explain."

"You're allowed," Mr. Johnson said with a grin on his face.

I laughed at his mannerism.

"Thank you kind sir. Like most things in life, bullying doesn't simply happening. There are deeper issues that are present, but not everyone acknowledges them because bullying is seen as such a despicable act. Everyone hates bullying; including the bully. In his mind;

he or she isn't the aggressor. They are simply reacting to something that has happened or is happening to them."

"How do you mean Doc? I've never heard of a bully beating up a kid that has done something to him. It's always the little kid that doesn't bother anyone that gets picked up," Mr. Johnson said.

"That's my point. The bully feels he is powerless to, for lack of a better word, attack those that cause him harm. So he finds someone that he feels is more powerless than him and they are subject to his aggression. The bully projects his anger and hurt unto them and attempts to create in them the same feelings he feels when he is being tormented. Are you familiar with the phrase; hurt people hurt people?"

Mr. Johnson exploded in laughter.

"I've heard that so many times, but I didn't understand it until now. I thought it was just something dumb people say trying to sound smart," Mr. Johnson said amidst hysterical laughter. "It actually makes sense now.

I laugh also. Mr. Johnson's laugh is contagious. He laughs in such a way that makes you feel that if you aren't laughing then it's something wrong with you.

"Don't feel bad," I say. "I've just now discovered the meaning of the phrase E for effort."

"What do you mean," Mr. Johnson asked amid laugher.

"I always thought E for effort meant the person failed miserably at whatever they were attempting to do, but because he tried he received an E instead of an F. I was recently told that the E was not a grade, but simply a mentioning of the first letter of the word," I said laughing." Mr. Johnson stated at me.

"Doc you might be the dumbest smart person I know."

I didn't know what to say; so I just decided to resume the previous conversation.

"As I was saying before; hurt people hurt people." Mr. Johnson sniggled.

"The physical and mental anguish bullies inflict on their victims is more indicative of what they're experiencing at home than it is about the delight they receive from tormenting others.
Mr. Johnson continued to drink his drink.

"What does that have to do with me Doc? I'm not a bully. My son isn't a bully. Are you saying that because I drink a lot? I don't get drunk and beat my son. Is that what you think doc?"

"I was getting to it before you cut me off."

"Well spit it out."
I smiled and paused for dramatic effect.

"Bullying was just an example I used to point out cause and effect. That's what we're really talking about."

"We ain't talking about shit." Mr. Johnson said. Making sure to place extra emphasis on we. "You're talking. I'm listening."

I smile. I could tell that Mr. Johnson was starting to feel the effects of his drinks.

"Ok," I say still smiling. "I was talking about cause and effect. I brought it up because I'm wondering what is the cause of your drinking."

"That's simple," Mr. Johnson said. "I like to drink."

"Would you drink if you never felt anything?"

"What do you mean?"

"I mean if there were no sensations that went along with drinking; would you continue to do it?"

Mr. Johnson looked at me with utter disdain.

"What kind of stupid ass question is that? What's the purpose of drinking if you can't feel the buzz?"

I smile.

"Well Mr. Johnson. You just admitted to not being addicted to alcohol itself, but to the feeling of being intoxicated."

"I can see that," Mr. Johnson said taking a sip.

"It is my belief that you've experienced traumatic events in your life that you haven't dealt with properly. The alcohol serves as a method for you to avoid the feelings that go along with those events."

"Right off Doc I can't think of anything. What about you?"

"I know what events caused me to use, but I don't know about you Mr. Johnson. That's what I'm asking." Mr. Johnson sat back on the couch and crossed his legs. He did this during our previous section. He calls it his thinking position.

"I don't know Doc. I can't think of anything. Why are you asking me anyway? You're asking me all these questions. What caused you to snort cocaine," he asked.

I could tell he was lashing out in an attempt to hurt my feelings. It didn't work.

"Because whatever has happened or didn't happen involved you. You're the best source of information regarding what we're discussing. I used cocaine when I was stressed or when I was partying or when I was bored or when the sun was shining or when it was raining. I used cocaine to live my life. I was suppressing my fear of success. Subconsciously I knew that I wouldn't be able to succeed while I was on drugs."
Mr. Johnson leaned forward.

"What do you mean your fear of success? I've heard of being afraid to fail, but never what you said. That must be some smart people shit."

"I was afraid to succeed because success would take me out of my comfort zone. I didn't want to have to deal with life outside of my comfort zone."

"That's deep Doc."

"Yes I know. It's deeper than what I've said, but we aren't here to talk about me. We're here to talk about you and what makes you drink."

"Shit Doc I don't know. That's why I came to you. For you to fix me."
I smile.

"Well Mr. Johnson. I don't fix people. I don't believe that people are broken. Damaged yes, but not broken. I need you to think for a second. What's happened that made you drink? Outside of the fact that you're always drinking."
He paused for a moment.

"I can't think of anything that happened to me directly."

"What do you mean?"

"One of my employees was going through something with his baby mama. I had to drink after hearing the story."

"What happened," I ask.

"I don't like telling other people's business Doc. That's gossiping. I'm a man and we don't gossip."

"I see your concern, however we aren't actually gossiping. I don't care to know the story, however if it's the only instance you can think of. I'm all ears."

"I won't say his name."

"That's perfectly fine."

"One of my employees was really messing up. Dropping tools, putting the wrong parts on cars and a host of other shit. I pull him aside because that's not like him. He's usually one of my best workers. Before I chew his ass out, I ask him what's going on. Man what I do that for? He starts telling me about issues he's having with his baby mama."

I cringe.

"What's wrong with you Doc," Mr. Johnson asks.

"I hate that term."

"What term, Mr. Johnson asked. On his face was a look of real confusion.

"Baby mama. Baby daddy too."

"Why?"

"I feel they diminish the person's role as a parent. Whether the person is living up to their duties or not; they should be called something better than baby daddy or baby mama. Then when you consider the stereotypes that associated with those words. It just bothers me."
Mr. Johnson shook his head.

"You're thinking too much Doc. It's not that serious, but I want say it if it bothers you that much. Can I finish my story now?"

"Yes please."

"Thank you. Like I was saying. He was having problems with his baby," he started. "My bad Doc. The mother of his child."

"Thank you."

"So he was trying to see his son. He asked if he could get her three weeks in advance. She said yes. They worked out a plan for him to get her. He was so excited. He wouldn't shut up about it. But apparently a week before he was supposed to get him; she texted him saying they don't feel comfortable allowing him to get him."

"Who's they," I ask.

"That's the same thing he asked. Apparently he never received an answer to that question. But to make a long story short; he was not able to get his son. After he told me that I had to go to the bar."

"You've never had that problem."

"What problem?"

"Not being able to see your son."

"Of course not. I married my woman so. Even If I didn't want him around; he'd be there."

"What did that remind you of?"

"What him not being able to get his son? Nothing. I never had that problem."

"I think you could relate him. The disappointment he felt. I think disappointment is one of your triggers."

"I don't have triggers. I just like to drink. And some situations I can't deal with while sober. That was one of them."

I smile.

"That's a trigger Mr. Johnson. When something happens that causes you to drink. We've discovered one of your triggers."

"So what do we do now? What's the first step?"

"Well Mr. Johnson, we're actually passed the first step. The second step also."

"Really? When the hell did that happen?"

"The first step was admitting you had a problem. The second step was seeking help. We're now at the third step."

Mr. Johnson finished his drink.

"What's that Doc?"

I glance at my watch.

"Calling you a cab so you can get home safely?"

"What?"

I look at him seriously.

"I cannot allow you to drive in your current condition. You're obviously beyond the legal limit. I'm proud of the progress we've made today, but I can't in good consciousness allow you to drive in your current condition."

Mr. Johnson laughed loudly.

"Oh shit Doc I may have a little buzz, but I'm far from drunk. A quick piss and I'm back to normal," Mr. Johnson said standing up. "Speaking of pissing; where's your bathroom. I have to drain the viper."

I laughed at his joke.

'The bathroom is out front in the receptionist area."

"Well Doc it's been real. Same time next week," he says reaching out to shake my hand.

"Yes sir," I say standing.

We shake hands and he heads towards the door. I watch him to see if he staggers at all. To my amazement; he doesn't. Not even a little bit.

"Amazing," I say aloud.

Chapter 9: Randy Roberts

After Mr. Johnson left; I sat in my office awaiting my final client of the day; Randy Roberts. He's been a patient for the last year. My initial encounter with Mr. Roberts was at The Harbor House Rehabilitation center. I was doing some free counseling and he was a patient there. He didn't seem to be a bad person and I could tell he desperately wanted to be living a sober life. During our last session he voiced his desire to continue our sessions; however he knew he would not be able to afford it. I made a deal with him; his sessions would be free as long as he remained free of any illegal substances. He promised he would and has yet to break his promise.

"Dr. Jenkins", Charlie says buzzing into my office. "Randy Roberts is here to see you."

"Ok Charlie. Send him in."

I was eager to meet with Mr. Roberts. He had been making excellent progress. So much so that he had developed a better relationship with his ex-wife and his daughter.

"Good Afternoon Mr. Roberts", I say as he walks into my office.

"Where's the liquor? I need a drink," he says ignoring my greetings.

"The decanter is empty, but I have an unopened bottle in the cabinet."

Mr. Roberts looked at me questionably. I could tell he wanted to know why the decanter was empty, but he didn't ask. He opened the bottle and took a rather large swig from the bottle. The size of the swig reminded me of Mr. Johnson.

"I hate her so much," he said in between swigs. M. Roberts only mentioned three women during his sessions; his daughter, his girlfriend, and his ex-wife. He had never spoken ill of his girlfriend or his daughter so I assumed he was talking about his ex-wife.

"Hate is such a strong word Mr. Roberts. We talked about finding other words to use to express how you feel. Who is she?"

"Who is she? The got damn devil. Regina. I know we talked about using other words, but the only word that properly sums up how I feel is hate. God. She makes me so angry. I wish all the bad things in the world happen to her and nobody else."

I smirk a little. I've heard people wish all manner of evil on others, but that was a new one. He was obviously talking about his ex-wife.

"She only angers you because you allow her to."

"Don't doctor me Dr. If I could kill her dog ass without going to jail; I'd do it. I promise I'd do it. Without hesitation," Mr. Roberts said taking his seat on the sofa.

"No you wouldn't Mr. Roberts. Doing so would not only lead you back to prison, but it would reverse all the progress you've made and cause your daughter to be placed in a foster home. "
Mr. Roberts didn't immediately respond. He just sat on the couch drinking from the bottle shaking his head.

"As much as I hate to admit it", He said eventually. "My daughter would be crushed if anything happened to her mom. She loves that woman."

"You would be equally as crushed."
Mr. Roberts laughed loudly.

"You must be the one on drugs now. If you think I would feel any pain if something happened to her," Mr. Roberts in-between bouts of laughter.

"You can laugh all you want Mr. Roberts but you and I both know the truth."

Mr. Roberts's laughter ceased.

"I don't know anything," He said.

"Yes you do. During our last session you praised her for prowess of a mother. You were almost swooning over the woman. This week it's something completely different. Why such a drastic change?"

"I'll tell you why. It all started when I texted her asking if I could get Clair."

I shook my head. Mr. Roberts's face turned red.

"I know you said not to text her, but I honestly hate hearing her voice."

"I have an idea as to why you hate her voice, but what's more important is the stark contrast in what you're saying today compared to what you said last week. You two were just on good terms."

"Just because we are on good terms doesn't mean I enjoy hearing her talk. It bothers me so much. And to be honest; I don't know why, but I hate hearing it. I know. She's bipolar. She needs to be sitting here too. "

"I'm interested in knowing how you think you two will ever properly co-parent? Or have a decent relationship? In order for things to work you're going to have to talk to her. "

"I hear what you're saying, but I'm not there yet. I'm working on it, but until that happens I'm looking for ways around that. I haven't come up with one yet though. But with us being on good terms I thought a cuick text message would be fine. So I sent the message expecting s simple yes or no."

Mr. Roberts shook his head.

"Judging by your reaction; I take it that her response wasn't a simple one, "I say.

"Not at all. I should have known it wasn't a simple response. It took her too long to respond. She sent a got damn essay about how I'm not going to be in and out of Claire's life and how she hasn't seen me since the beginning of last year. Which was a lie. She said that I've been neglecting her since she was born. Then went on to say that I need to send her a list of dates for the month of when I'm going to see her. Basically make appointments to see my own child. I don't understand where she gets off telling me these things. Especially since we were just cool."

"Weren't you in and out of her life at one point," I asked.

"Yes, but that's when I was on drugs. I'm sober now. I'm better, progressing, getting things in order. Instead of making things harder; she should be helping. If not helping directly at least not make things more difficult. And stop lying on me."

I smile.

"What exactly would you like for her to do," I ask. Mr. Richards paused for a moment. I could tell he was thinking long and hard about what I asked. I decided to give him more things to think about.

"The thing is Mr. Richards," I say taking off my glasses. "You're actually to blame for how your ex-wife is behaving. To go deeper into what I'm saying; you feel that you two are on good terms when she is acting like the person you fell in love with opposed to the person you've made her become."
He looked at me with a mixture of disgust and confusion.

"Allow me to explain," I continued. "Men influence women a lot more than we realize or that they will admit to. We teach them how to treat us. It's not a conscious thing. Our habits, speech patterns, and the things we do and don't do all play a part in their behavior. Are you with me so far?"

"Yes. I've heard that before but I don't see how I taught her to disrespect me and constantly ridicule me."

"I'm getting there. I just need you follow along. During previous sessions you admitted to being a deadbeat dad. Do you remember that?"

"Yes I remember saying that. I wasn't a deadbeat by choice. I was on drugs then. I'm off now though. I wouldn't say I was neglecting her though."

"One can argue that you made the choice to be a deadbeat. When you chose to engage in drug usage; you made the decision to neglect your child. Neglect is simply not paying attention to something or someone. So you in actuality you have neglected her. I wouldn't go as far as to say her entire life, but definitely a great majority of it."
I paused to allow my words to sink in. I thought he would have something to say, however he did not.

"Resuming my original statement," I say. "There was an extended period of time where you were extremely unreliable. Is that correct?"

"Yes, but I'm not like that anymore."

"You keep saying that. Are you trying to convince me that you've changed or are you justifying your past behaviors," I ask rhetorically. "As I was saying; majority of your child's life you've been an unreliable drug addict."

"Ouch man. Tell me how you really feel," Mr. Roberts said.

"I am," I say back. "Back to what happened. While you were an active drug addict; life was happening for your now ex-wife and your daughter. Your then wife had to bear the blunt of responsibilities for the child you two created together while simultaneously dealing with the effects of your drug addiction; the arrests, the missing for days at a time, you spending bill money on drugs, and all the other things she had to deal with that was a direct result of your drug usage. Not to mention the heartache she had to endure seeing the person she loves be on drugs. I can say that she may be acting that way because she feels anger because you're getting your life together now. While you're dating another women. She may feel jealousy because you didn't do that with her; however that alleviates you of blame. That's not why we are here. We are here to help you. We can't do that pointing blame anywhere else."

Mr. Roberts was silent for a moment.

"When I got out of rehab I've apologized for that. Multiple times," he said.

"How many times did you apologize during your addiction?"

"Countless, but I told her I would be better."

"During your drug addiction; how many times did you tell her you would do better?"

"But I told her I quit."

"How many times did you tell her you quit only to resume using?"

"Many, but I mean it this time. I've never been clean for this long. It's been a whole year."

"That's true Mr. Roberts. No one can take that from you. I proud of you for not doing any drugs. For an entire year. I understand how difficult it was. Please keep up the good work."
Mr. Roberts looked proud of himself. I debated how I would continue the conversation. If I would allow him to feel good about himself or attack that confidence to build him up later.

"The thing is Mr. Roberts," I began. "You were in active addiction a lot longer than you've been sober. You're going to have to work extremely hard to reverse the negative effects your behavior caused. Have you been doing that?"

"Yes," Mr. Richards said.

"What have you been doing?"

"I call Claire, spend time with her when I can, and I even send her money when I can."

"You told me you did those things occasionally when you were high."

"Yes that's true."

"Well Mr. Richards, what's different now?"

"My motive. I do those things now because I want to. Because I'm supposed to. I'm supposed to take care of Claire. And the frequency I do things.

"In essence Mr. Roberts, you're still doing the things you did when you were in active addiction. When is the last time you spent time with Claire?"
Mr. Richards seem to think for a moment.

"About two months ago," he said.

"When is the last time you sent money?"

"Around the same time."

I didn't say anything. I just looked at him. Mr. Richards looked at the floor.

"Why are you coming down on me so heavily," Mr. Richards asked. "You're making it seem like I haven't made any headway."

"It's not that you haven't made any, but you haven't made as much as you think."

"Say something nice."
His words made me laugh a little.

"I apologize for laughing," I say. "My daughter says that to her mother whenever she's being fussed at. At any rate. Something nice. In my opinion you've made the most important step."

"What's that? Coming to see you," Mr. Roberts said sarcastically.

"No. Coming to see me is the second most important step," I say returning his sarcasm. "The most important step was to stop doing drugs. I actually admire you for that. I understand how difficult that was, but you overcame that."

Mr. Richards looked at me with hope in his eyes.

"But Mr. Richards," I continue. If you continue to consume alcohol in the manner in which you do; it's just a matter of time before you're back getting high."

"You're right. I don't like drinking, but she makes me so angry. I can't help it."

"You need to. You have to learn to control your emotions and reactions. You need more self-restraint. If you can't soberly deal with her attitude; you're going to end up back on drugs. Do you understand?"

"Yes," he said.

"Good. Changing subjects. How's that beautiful girlfriend of yours doing," I ask smiling.

Mr. Richards's frowned at me.

Chapter 10: Randy Roberts II

"Why do you ask that," Mr. Roberts asked.

"Because I want to know."

"She's fine."

I could tell me asking about Michelle made me anxious. I wanted to know why.

"Mr. Roberts, what's on your mind," I asked."

"I just told you."

"No. We talked about what was on your mind. I'm asking what is currently on your mind."

Mr. Roberts sighed.

"Michele has an event to attend tonight," he finally said.

"Congratulations."

Mr. Roberts looked at me with a confused expression.

"Continue please," I say before he could ask any questions.

"She has another one of those uppity events. You know the ones that lawyers, doctors, and those kinds of people go to."

"A networking event."

"Yes. Networking," Mr. Roberts said using air quotes.

"I take it you don't enjoy going to those events."

"Not at all doctor."

"Why not? Is it because you're not considered a professional?'

"No I just don't like being around those people."

"Have you told Michelle?"

"Yes."

"What did she say?"

"She told me to stay home."

"Well there you go."

"I can't let her go alone."

"Why can't you?"

Mr. Roberts didn't say anything. He just looked into the distance. The expression on his face indicated that he was trying to find the right words to use.

"Because", he finally started. "There are a lot of black people there."

"There are a lot of black people on Earth. Michelle being one of them."

"Yes I know, but."

Mr. Roberts paused.

"Go on", I encouraged.

"I don't mean to sound racist."

"I'm not concerned about if you sound racist. Sounding racist isn't a problem. Speak freely Mr. Roberts and tell me exactly how you feel."

"So at these events there are all these black professionals as you call them. They graduated from college are doing well financially and have their lives on track," Mr. Roberts said.

I could tell he was trying his hardest to not sound racist.

"Continue Mr. Roberts," I say.

"I don't fit in with them. They are all friendly with one another. They seem to share a bond. There's an admiration they have for each other. I guess because they have overcome a lot to get where they are or whatever, but I feel left it. It's like there's a joke that I'm not a part of."

I knew he had more to say so I didn't respond.

"I'm not the only that feels like that. The others feel like that too," Mr. Roberts continued. "There are three of us. Surrounded by a sea of blackness."

"When you say three of us; what do you mean?"
Mr. Roberts looked at me.

"White people."

"It's the same people all the time?"

"Yes for the most part."

"When you're there; do you talk to any people of color?"

"Yes of course. I talk to Michelle's boss and her friends are all great people. Great women. I could talk to them for hours."

"What about her male colleagues?"
Mr. Roberts face turned red.

"What about them," He asked.

"Do you interact with them?"

"No not really," Mr. Roberts said looking at the ground.
I smiled.

"So you're comfortable engaging with her female colleagues, but not the males."

"I wouldn't phrase it like that."

"How would you phrase it?"

"It just so happens that the people I'm most comfortable with happen to be women."

"Are you like that with all races?"

"What do you mean?"

"Exactly what I said. Are you more comfortable with women of other races than you are men of other races?"

Mr. Roberts appeared to be thinking.

"No. It's about the same."

I smile.

"So how long have you hated black men?"

All the blood appeared to leave Mr. Roberts faces. I thought he might pass out.

"I don't hate black men," Mr. Roberts said clearly flustered.

"I think you do."

"I don't. Why would you say such a thing?"

"Because it's the truth. Based on what you've said."

"It's not the truth. Is that what you think?"

"Here's what I think. I think you see black men, more specifically professional black men, as a threat to your way of life."

"That's outrageous," Mr. Roberts said interrupting. I smile.

"We can sing together, however we cannot talk together. Allow me to finish my thought."

"Ok."

"I think you see black men as a threat to the life you hope to build with Michelle."

"What do you mean?"

"I'm glad you asked. Those black men represent the manifestation of your subconscious fears. They are better, dress better, more intelligent, and more successful. Not to mention the fact that they share something with Michelle that you could never share. Melanin. To you; that's what her ideal mate would look like."

"I don't think I'm ugly or unsuccessful. Or dumb"

"I didn't say you did. I said you feel they are more adept in those areas."

I paused for a moment to allow my words to sink in and to study Mr. Roberts face. He looked like his deepest darkest secret had been exposed for the world to see   His facial expression was a combination of shame, anger, and hopelessness. I decided to keep pushing.

"You have convinced yourself that black men can offer Michelle a better life than the one you can. Let's face it. They have more things in common with her. They are bigger and stronger and more likely to keep her safer than you can. Not to mention the stereotype that black men are better equipped for sexual activities.

Mr. Roberts looked like he might be sick. I decided to be silent for a moment.

"It's not fair." Mr. Roberts said so low it was almost a whisper.

"What's not fair," I ask.

"That they are more well off than I am. I'm supposed to be the one that's rich and handsome and desirable. Not them. I'm not supposed to be feeling this way."

"What way is that?"

"You've already said it."

"I want you to say it."

Mr. Roberts looked up at me momentarily but quickly resumed looking at the floor.

"Feeling like I'm hopeless. Feeling like the men in that room can provide a better life for Michelle."

"Not just the men in that room," I say. "All successful black men."

"All successful black men."

"How can they provide her a better life?"

"They could buy her things and relate to her in ways that I can't. There are moments where she makes reference to this show called Martin. Have you heard of it?"
I laugh a little.

"Yes I've heard of it."

"Apparently it's supposed to be a great show, but I've never seen it. I can't relate to the jokes. I can't relate to her struggles. I don't know what to say in moments where she wants to discuss discrimination, racism or ways to improve the black community."
Mr. Roberts is nearly in tears.

"So why don't you let her go?" Allow one of the more suitable black men to have her."

"Because I can't," Mr. Roberts yells. "I need her. She's the only reason I've been able to remain sober this long. She's my everything. I can't lose her."

"Do you think you will?"

"If I do; it'll be to one of the black men at those events. I just know it. I wish there was a way to keep her from going to those events. Keep those men away from her."

"What are you thinking?"

"I don't know. I can't fight all of them. They'd kill me. I don't know what to do. I'm powerless."

"Powerless," I ask.

"Yes powerless. There's nothing I can do. If one of them takes her," Mr. Robert said shaking his head. "I'm as good as dead. I know it. I'm going to get back on drugs real bad. I will OD not long after. I'm going to die."

"So what you're saying is that your very survival is contingent upon separating Michelle from black men."

"I didn't mean it like that."

"Yes you did. You used a lot of unnecessary words, but the meaning was clear. You feel that you are inferior to black men. Especially successful black men. You fear that they will cause you to lose your life. So in order for you to survive you must eliminate the threat. You can't physically, and don't have the power structure to do so economically so your only option is to separate her from them. Remove her from their world. In essence what's happening is a white man sees a black man as a threat and seeks to eliminate the threat."

"I'm not racist."

"I didn't say you were."

"Yes you did," Mr. Roberts says jumping to his feet.

"No I said you're a white man that sees black men as a threat to his livelihood and is seeking to eliminate the threat."

"That's what a racist is."

"Yes that's true, but I didn't use the word racist."

"You didn't have to. It was implied."

"So using a lot of unnecessary words to express my thought is the same as directly saying what I mean?"
Mr. Roberts looked at the ground. He didn't say anything. He must have known where I was going.

"One of my favorite historical people, Dr. Frances Cress-Welsing says that racism developed out of white man's fear of extinction. The same fear you've expressed today.

"I'm not a racist," Mr. Roberts said exhaustedly. "The love of my life is black."
I smile.

"You know all racists allude to having a black friend. Dylan Roof had a black friend too."
Mr. Roberts shook his head.

"I can't believe you compared me to that monster," Mr. Roberts said. "He slaughtered innocent people. I could never do that."

"I was simply showing you a correlation. Saying you have a black friend or in your case, being in love with a black person doesn't disqualify you from being racist." He looked at me with a confused expression on his face.

"Well what does it do? How do I prove I'm not racist? There was a look of genuine concern on his face. I could tell he was adamant about not appearing to be a racist.

"The way you prove you're not a racist is by not being a racist," I say.

"That's easier said than done. You people are so sensitive to that sort of thing."

"You are aware that referring to black people as 'you people' is extremely racist right?" He threw his hands up in exasperation.

"See I can't win. Everything I say can be misconstrued as being racist."

"Yes but only because you're a racist," I say

Mr. Roberts's face turns a bright shade of red.

"I know you're going to say that you aren't a racist, however let's pose it this way. Is it really just wrong for you people to be racists?"

"You said 'you people'.

"Yes I know. I did so purposefully. I said it to separate white people from the rest of humanity."

"That's not right," Mr. Roberts said.

"Well you said it to me. It has to be ok because you said it. Regardless of how it made me feel it was ok because you say you had no malicious intent.

Mr. Roberts didn't say anything. I sat quietly for a few moments. Giving him the opportunity to process what I said and to allow him to wallow in my words.

"As I was saying," I continue. "Isn't it in white people's best interests to be racist, oppressive monsters? Especially when you consider the fact that white people are the minority on Earth."

"No we aren't. There are more whites than blacks, Mexicans, Africans, and Asians."

I smile. I'm relishing at the opportunity I've been given to educate Mr. Roberts.

"Yes whites are more numerous than those groups individually, however when combined; whites are significantly outnumbered."

Mr. Roberts was visibly confused.

"Follow me Mr. Roberts. Instead of dividing the groups by country, religion, language or culture; let's divide the people into two groups; those with a significant amount of melanin and those without it."

"Melanin," Mr. Roberts said.

"Yes melanin. You are aware of what that is right?"

He glared at me.

"Yes, it's what makes black people black."

"It's more than that. I don't have time to go into an in-depth discussion of what it is and what it does so for sake of this conversation; we'll say that melanin is what gives people their color."

"I thought only black people had melanin," he asked.

"No sir. All people have melanin; however blacks have the highest concentration of it."
He nodded to indicate he understood what I was saying.

"So with white people being in the group with the lowest concentration of melanin and their genes being recessive, and their population dwindling; doesn't it make sense for them to be racist? To favor people that look like them in hopes to keep their numbers up?"
He didn't say anything.

"That wasn't a rhetorical question Mr. Roberts. I'm interested to know your thoughts."

"I hear what you're saying, but there are ways to go about preserving the race. We don't have to put people down or discriminate against them. We can thrive without all that. "

"Great answer Mr. Roberts. I don't think you're racist, but you have the potential to be. You need to get that under control."

"How do I do that," Mr. Roberts asked.
I smile.

"Well Mr. Roberts I'd tell you, but unfortunately today's session has come to an end. I'll see you next week."

Chapter 11: Ole girl At the Bus Station

After making notes about Mr. Robert's session; I gather my things to leave.

"I'll see you tomorrow Charlie," I say walked passed her desk. "Call me if you need me."

"I can't believe you're actually leaving before 5:00. This has to be a record."

We both laugh. I pull out my phone to text my wife.

"I'm headed home," I say.

"What? Dr. Jenkins will be home before the sun goes down? You must've gotten fired. LOL."

"LOL. NO mam. I just miss my wife."

"I see you flirting with me. Hurry home please."

"Yes mam."

The bus stop isn't far from the office. In no time I am standing with the rest of those that utilize of the public bus system. Unfortunately the bench is full so I have to stand. I knew I wouldn't be able to comfortably engage in my favorite past time, people watching. I didn't fret about it because I had been sitting all day.

Everyone was pre-occupied with their own lives; with the exception of one young man. I notice that he's been staring at one young lady since I've arrived. She hasn't noticed. She's been staring at her phone the entire time. Watching the young man I could tell he was trying to find the courage to approach the young lady.

"Excuse me," he says.

She didn't respond. Either she didn't hear him or she's great at ignoring people. My guess is that it's a combination of both.

"Excuse me," he says again. Louder this time.

"Yes," she says seductively.

The young man smiles awkwardly. I think his mind went blank.

"Ummmm. My name is Michael. What's your name?"

"Brittany," she says.

The man paused. It appears he's run out of things to say. Hopefully he finds the words to say. I'm rooting for him.

"You're really pretty and I would love the opportunity to build with you," he said nervously. Brittany smiled.

"I don't think so," she said coldly.

"Why not?"

"Umm how do I say this? You can't afford to date a person like me."
Utter confusion ran across Michael's face. I too was a bit confused about what she meant.

"What do you mean afford," he asked. "Are you a prostitute?"

"Is your mama a prostitute," she asked angrily.

"I wasn't trying to offend you. You said afford so I thought you were for sale."

Brittany rolled her eyes. By this time everyone was watching their exchange.

"If I was for sale your broke ass couldn't afford me."

"What makes you think I'm broke?"

"Umm let's see. Your shoes are cheap. Don't nobody wear Reeboks no more. We wear red bottoms, Gucci, Louie. Stuff like that and you're on the bus. Boy bye. Get out my face. You've wasted enough of my time," she said matter of factly.

"Damn," the guy standing beside me said.

"I know right," a woman with dreads said. "She didn't have to do him like that."

Brittany flashed a fake smile and returned to her phone. Judging by his facial expression; Michael didn't know what to say or do. He just stood there. Looking at her. She eventually looked up from her phone to see him still standing there.

"Can I help you," she said irritably.

"No I'm good."

"So," she said rolling her neck. "Can you move? I don't want people thinking we are together."

Michael looked like he lost his best friend. I laughed a little. I don't usually feel bad for people; however he had just experienced an unnecessarily harsh tongue lashing. He walked away from her. As he was walking away the bus arrived.

He was the first to get on the bus. Ashley was right behind him. It wasn't extremely packed, however there weren't many seats. I saw that Ashley was sitting alone.

"Excuse me Ms," I say smiling. "Do you mind if I sit here?"

"I do but I don't own the bus so do whatever you want," she says not looking up from her phone.

I take a seat. I never understood why people were so infatuated by their cell phones. They are control by that little box. The world outside the phone is much more interesting.

Take the couple sitting on the seats in front of me. They're obviously trying to hide the fact that they are fighting, however they are failing miserably. The looks she is giving him should be illegal. He's looking at her just as angrily. After few minutes we come to a stop. Michael walks past us. I hear Brittany say something.

"What was that," I say turning to face her.

"Oh. I wasn't talking to you."

"Yes I know, however that doesn't negate the fact that I want to know what you said."
She rolled her eyes.

"Well if you must know," She said. "I called that guy that walked by a loser."

"Why would you do that? What makes him a loser?"

She looked at me for a moment. Judging by the look on her face she was trying to decide if she would answer my question or curse me out.

"He's broke," she finally said.

"Oh. You know him personally."

"Naw not really. I just met him about thirty minutes ago."

"So how do you know he's broke?"

"Why are you asking me all these questions?" I don't know you.

I smile.

"Where are my manners? My name is Dr. James Jenkins. I'm a psychiatrist. I'm asking these questions because I have an affinity for how people interact with one another. Often times that interaction comes in the form of verbal and nonverbal ques. As well as assumptions we make about one another. I apologize for the questions."

I noticed that her eyes lit up when I mentioned I was a doctor. Undoubtedly she didn't hear anything else I said.

"It's ok doctor," she said smiling hard.

"Good. Back to the gentlemen I asked about," I say. "How do you know he's broke?"

"I just know. I can spot a broke dude a mile away. Look at how he carries himself. And he's on the bus." I look at her with confusion.

"I know I'm on the bus too," she says. "But I'm going through a transitional period. I can't date someone who's going through the same struggle as me."

"That actually makes sense."

"I know it does. He doesn't have what it takes to date me."

"What does it take to date you?" Ashley smiles.

"Depends on who's asking," she says.

"I would think your requirements would remain constant regardless of who's asking, but for conversation's sake let's say Christian Johnson from Canton, MS."

"Hmm," she says. "Well off top I feel like the only reason he's trying to talk to me is to get some so he's going to have to come off them coins. I need my hair done, my nails done, and I need shopping trips and dates," Ashley said with her head cocked to the side.

"Wow that's a lot."

"Ain't nothing in life free. You have to pay for what you want."

"Well the thing is Christian Johnson from Canton Ms doesn't have time to put in the effort necessary to do all those things. He's a busy man and refuses to waste time on someone he can't build with. So he presents you with this proposition; He will give you the money so you can get your hair and nails done, go shopping and go on dates; however he's trying to smash tonight."

"What," Brittany said loudly.

"Christian Johnson from Canton Ms is trying to give you the money up front so he can smash. He doesn't want to waste his time or your time."

"I ain't no hoe," Brittany yells.

I smile.

"Are you sure," I ask. "You just said that a man has to spend money on you before you'll have sex with him. Is that not what hoes do? Take money in exchange for their time."

"Yes, but that's over a period of time."

"Christian Johnson from Canton, MS doesn't have time to spend with a person he's only going to have sex with. No emotional attachment. That's what you said."

Ashley looked out the window.

"I ain't no hoe, she said.

I noticed that her voice cracked when she said it.

"Who are you trying to convince," I ask. "Me or

you?"

"Who the hell do you think you are," Ashley yelled.

"Judge me like you're some type of saint of something.

You don't know me. You don't know my life."

I look around and see people watching us. I smile and nod

at them before returning my attention to Ashley.

"I've been through a lot of shit," she continues.

"You don't know me. You don't know what it's like not

knowing who your father is or if your mom loves you. Or if

anyone loves you for that matter. So if a dude wants to

sleep with me he's going to have to pay. If he wants my

time. He's going to have to pay. I refuse to be taken

advantage of or mistreated and left for broke. Not me.

That's not going to happen to me."

I could tell she was trying to fight back tears. It was

evident that this young lady had a rough time growing up

and our conversation was bringing back memories. I was curious to know exactly what she had been through.

"What happened to you," I ask.

"What do you mean?"

Her eyes were glistening.

"I mean exactly what I said. What happened to you?"

"Nothing happened to me."

"That's not true mam. It's evident that you've experienced a traumatic event. Judging by the tears in your eyes; I'd say it was more than one."

She didn't say anything. She just looked out the window. I waited for her to respond.

"Why do you care," she said.

She was still looking out the window.

"Why I care isn't nearly as important as the fact that I care."

She sucked her teeth.

"I'm listening," I say.

I didn't want to press the issue. She shook her head.

"I can't believe I'm about to tell you this, but I was raped. By my mama's brothers."

"Your uncles?"

"No. My mama's brothers. They're not related to me. They're dead to me."
She wiped her eyes. "No relative would do that to someone they're related to."

"I was twelve the first time it happened."

"So it happened multiple times."

"Yes," She said looking at me. "It happened at nearly every family function until I was fourteen."
I shake my head in disguise. I detest people that prey on children.

"What did your mother say when she found out," I ask.

"That bitch thought I was lying," She said angrily. "She didn't want to believe that they were capable of doing anything wrong. After all, they raised her and she turned out ok. She's dead to me too."

"That's terrible. A mother that doesn't believe her child when she says she was raped was raped herself." She looked at me.

"In my experiences that's been the case," I say.

"She should've told me that. That would have made me feel so much better. To have someone to share what I went through with that's also gone through it. Man."

I shrug. She resumed looking out the window.

"She made me have an abortion," she says.

"They impregnated you?

"Yes. And my mother made me get an abortion. Talking about it would make her look bad if her daughter ended up pregnant. I wanted to have the baby. To prove to her that I had been telling the truth the entire time. To show

her what her brothers had been doing to me. Maybe then

she would be on my side. And support me."

"So why have the abortion," I ask.

"She made me. She said she wouldn't help me. And

that she would put me out the house. I couldn't raise a baby

alone. Not at that age."

"Do you have any kids now?"
She hesitated.

"I can't have kids," she says solemnly.

"I'm sorry," I say. "I don't usually feel sorry for

people, however you fall into one of the categories of

people that get my sympathy."

"Categories of people," she asked.
There was a look of confusion on her face.

"Yes. I only feel sorry for crack babies and rape

victims."

"What the hell? Why?"

"Because those two categories of people had no power to control what happened to them. They are complete victims."

"WOW. Never thought of that."

"I know. Fortunately my stop is coming up so I must cut the conversation short, but you need me," I say reaching into the inner pocket of my suit jacket. "Here's my card. Call my assistant to set up an appointment."

"I don't need a shrink." She says snatching the card out my hand.

I smile standing up.

"No one wants one, but you need one," I say exiting the bus. "You can bring your mother too."